YOU

James Colbourne

Esc publishers

Part One

One

Last week, you had a tail. This week, you are the same size as a raspberry. Last year, you were a dream. Last week, I dreamt you were a girl, embracing me, your skin on mine. Next week, you'll be a little bigger. Maybe the size of a strawberry. I don't know. In seven months' time, I pray, we'll say Hello to each other, on your birthday (maybe a week after mine). And today? Today, you lie warm and snug, we hope. You, you, you.

And me, I'm wondering whether or not I'm a Daddy. Do I have the courage to call myself that yet? You're a dream come true and the most precious and precocious thing I could ever dream of imagining. So much so, that the very thought of you sends an almighty thunderclap up my spine. Maybe you know that we are all prone to exaggeration sometimes. But I swear to whoever/whatever will listen/is listening that I am not this time. With all the strength I can muster I'll call myself Daddy for just a little while. You, you, you.

You're with Mommy in a car on the way to a small city called Hof. And I'm scribbling tiny blue words in a small place called Naila. Soon I'll eat what Nanny has cooked for me. We'll talk again after I've eaten, if you don't mind. Okay?

You now? I don't know. Maybe 10, 15, 18, 21. As you read now, I can't imagine. Only last week we found out in this very room I write in now, in fact. A quiet, whispered secret you were then, and now too. I've changed from the desk to the dinner table, I write with a Holiday Inn Express pen (we stayed there last week, I think, as did you, I suppose...) on plain paper from a printer. Pepper the cat is feverishly licking herself, blissfully unaware that I'm writing my first ever letters to my son or daughter (delete as appropriate, sorry). Oh, the life of a cat. German television is on in the background, I'm trying to ignore it. Nanny/Granny/Großmutter/Petra just asked me what I was writing. I fumblingly said it was "kind of like a diary, just something... Not much... and, uhm, ...". I've always written something: Poems, short stories, even two novels, once upon a time. But I've never written to someone like you, an unborn baby, a marvellous secret, mine and Mommy's 'thing'. Even that word seems strange: Mommy. Yet if you are a you, and you certainly are now, causing sickness and weight, soreness and tiredness (I'm sorry, no guilt trip intended). Not to mention whispers, kisses, dreams, plans. Possibilities.

It's hard for me to get all of these words out. Perhaps a poem? Here we go. I wrote it the day we found out, in the front seat of a car, on the road as always. How many raspberry-sized beings get a poem? Sorry for the title, it's 'Untitled penguin hiiid'.

Yesterday was the news
The blurry line and the red line
And now these scribbled scruffy
Words are for you

I'm scared to call me Daddy
Until Mommy is Mommy
And you are you
Hope is a fickle thing
Forever slippy and unforeseen

Yet you I suppose are you
Right now like a piece of rice

A fragile thought
A piece of us
We need to find you fast, unfrozen

I know where you are
Count to one hundred and find me
And we'll play the game.
I'm telling myself I am me
There's a we
And now there's you.

So, like I said, sorry about the title. I've made a point of not changing it, they were just my half-thought ramblings as we rumbled down another Autobahn. It started off all negative, frightened and unsure, uncertain, un-everything really. And then I tried to summon up the positivity I hide sometimes to try and convince myself that you are real. You'll be even 'realer', but you're real now. Last week in a hot salty swimming pool, I added to it, with a few tears, telling your Ma my fears, concerns and doubts. No doubt getting something (whatever 'it' was) off my chest. Of course, blurry and red lines are from the pregnancy test. One already on there in bright red and then another to show a sign of life to come. She brought it to me, I was still on the sofa bed we had slept on the night before, and we had both slept badly. Thinking of the morning, I'm sure. My first reaction should have been screaming or yelling or dancing a crazed Charleston on your Grandmother's sofa, but I couldn't believe that faint line was real. Even now, a week later, I can't describe it adequately. Maybe the best moments, or the most momentous moments in our lives are indescribable, always. Like I said to your Ma, I was like a man who has won the lottery and he keeps on checking the ticket, in disbelief at his luck.

In just a few days, we'll see you for the first time, and this man for whom religion has often passed by will be praying all of that time that everything is okay. Happy, healthy, four limbs, ten toes, ten fingers, whether boy or girl, we don't mind really. And then, and then you, you, you can complete the circles in my mind, can allow a thousand smiles as we tell everyone those magic words 'We're pregnant'. You can bring kisses, embraces, hands held, parties, presents, cards. You can make your Ma a Ma, me a Papa, Nannies Nannies and Granddads Granddads. No pressure. You will have one uncle and one cousin. The rest of them you'll figure it out. But for now, let me ask you the favour of being. Right now I'm sure I seem a man of many words, but really it's just an attempt to find the *right* words. Call it what you will: a diary, a letter, a prayer.

I want to write to you, I'll simply talk to you and tell you that we love you. In fact, the last few weeks have seen me, each night, talking to and kissing the belly you are in, wishing you good night and telling you that we love you. Just think of these words like that, an extension of a bewildered and happy man's words to his unborn. You, you, you.

As for today, Nanny and Mommy are ill, while I write these lines. Nanny is no doubt a little confused as to why exactly I'm filling pages with blue biro ink, but Oh well, perhaps I can tell her next week. Don't forget, you don't have to wave at us when the time comes, but a healthy heartbeat and only one head, well, that would be nice.

The cat is now asleep, dreaming catty dreams; chasing mice, besting dogs, eating fish, etc. The TV is playing a little background music, making me think of another night last week, on the way back to Naila, from near Mannheim, after we had visited Jan, your cousin. Many,

many hours we drove down the darkened motorways, winding our way home. I sat in the back, caught between slumber and thought, listening to my MP3 player (a gift from your Ma). I don't mind admitting again that a few little drops fell from my eyes. Thank god you exist in a world now in which a man can admit these things, it hasn't always been the case. Many hours we drove and I don't think you left my thoughts for more than two minutes. It was before 'the test', before the step towards a new life. You were only a fragile hope of ours, as you are right now a tiny fragile thing inside another person. The next day, I knew we would find out one way or another. I sat there, a mind burdened with hope and hindered by the possibility of... nothing, a negative. And now, and now? You, you, you. Thank you.

Pepper is trying to eat these pages, she's taken a sudden dislike to page number six in particular. Sitting on the table minding its own business it was, and then a sudden vicious feline attack. I took a picture, I doubt if I still have it now though.

I've written a lot tonight. Let me let you talk. Here are some questions for you to answer if and when you may happen to read this. In my work now that's kind of what I do, ask questions. I think a good teacher should know when to shut the hell up and let the student talk. Hey, wake up, you there at the back! Are you left-handed like me? Have you got stuck-to-the-head ears like your Ma? A boy like me? A girl like your Ma? Patient like me? Smart like your Ma? Good at music? Sports? Like travelling? Like reading? I hope you take after us with that (for your sake).

Whatever you do, however you are, whatever does or does not happen, know always that you are a dream come true. Ta-ra. Speak soon. You, you, you.

Two

Back in Rome, sat at a piano, unable to play it. So am instead talking to you again and your Ma is reading the pregnancy book we bought in England. About what food she can eat, and the possibility of twins. As you may or may not, in fact, be two people right now instead of the traditional one. Your Granddad Roland is a twin and they say that it skips a generation, so the possibility remains that while I write to you there could be two pairs of ears listening in. Please do try to be nice to each other, if that is the case. Personally, I doubt it.

Again, I dreamed of you last night, this time you were a boy. Last night, we raced two plastic little penguins along the kitchen floor and picked one as a boy and one as a girl. Yes, this is the kind of thing your parents were doing before you were born. Hard to imagine, I suppose. Again, she is bombarding me with terrible girls' names. Sheila and Genevieve were the latest two. Don't worry, I'm fighting hard for a good name. Unfortunately, we keep on picking common ones for a girl. Emily, Yasmin and Olivia are the top three at the moment. And if it's a boy, we are fairly stuck on Samuel, who, I'm sure you know by now, is your Great-Grandfather's name.

"Choosing nappies".
She said randomly to me just three and a half seconds ago, and that's another battle I must endeavour to be triumphant in.
"Can you tell them to start using the potty soon, please?"

I think she just read that some kids are still wearing nappies at two or three years old.
Please don't let me still be wiping your bottom when you're three, okay? Deal? You can have any Christmas present you want. Deal? Okay. These are the things we are talking about now in our apartment in Rome. Names, nappies, new horizons. Oh, and by the way, I was right, you are now the size of a strawberry at ten weeks. Who knows how big you'll be next Monday. They say that in the next three weeks you will double in size and right this minute you have fingernails. It's hard to imagine a strawberry-sized baby with fingernails.

And if doubt is still lingering in the air this evening, it's because we thought we might have had our first real glimpse of you today. We called the doctor's this morning and fixed an appointment for 5:30. They cancelled it. I met your Ma and we went shopping instead. We rescheduled for Tuesday, that's four whole days away. They say that a so-called 'dating scan' should be done around twelve weeks. There's so much I can't wait for, culminating in the first real 'real' appearance which we think could be at the end of July. But right now I'm hoping and hoping that on Tuesday we can see you and count the four limbs, ten fingers, ten toes, and most importantly, see the tiny heart beating. And then to tell my parents, on Skype, on my little tablet computer. Their smiles will fill up the little screen. By now I suppose you know they couldn't have their 'own' children and that's why they adopted me.

We'll tell them as soon as we can. And Petra and Roland and David too. I'm working at an Italian school right now, teaching English, and I'm working on a way to finish early on Tuesday, so I can be with your Ma for the appointment. Don't worry, I'll be there. I'll see you on a screen hopefully, but you won't be able to see us yet.

They'll put some cold gel on your Ma's stomach and then press it with some sort of device that lets the doctor see inside the belly. Where you are now.

Your Ma is still not feeling very well, not because of you, it's a cold she can't seem to shake off. She's lying on our big sofa in the same room as me, we're talking a little while I write. She's got a big white blanket covering her legs, trying to keep herself warm. She's not really showing the pregnant belly just yet, that will come in the next few weeks I imagine. We've not long finished dinner. Pepper is under the blanket, equal parts cuddly-cute and vicious-scratchy-bity-wannabe tiger. Today, I've been reading a book of poetry again and I thought maybe it would rub off on me a little bit, instead, I feel like I'm having a funny little one-sided conversation. How I wish I could talk to you for real, pick you up, kiss you, hug you, read you a story, feed you, anything. Tonight again I'll talk to a stomach, with all the good-will in the world inside of me. If your Ma is carrying you and doing all the hard work, what else should I do? For you we would both move heaven and earth but right now I'm so impatient. Tuesday feels like a century away.

You are worth waiting for though, I'm sure, and boy or girl or even twins, right now, reading this at whatever age you are, I hope I'm not boring you and I hope you are happy and healthy. To be wealthy and wise? Well, that would be nice too, but despite my impatience and moaning, I'm not a greedy man.

By the way, your Ma's penguin won (the girl one) so now we think you'll be a girl anyway. Tell me if I'm wrong. So many thoughts, concerns and dreams we have for you. Uncertainty breeds questions which grow and escalate in answers we don't have. A plan we have right now is to take you to France, England, and Germany after you're born and have had a week or two in Rome first. Who knows how that will go? Our fate is in the hands of your destiny. Even now, as I write, we bicker mildly about whether or not she will ski soon. Only a little bickering, don't worry. Now in the unforeseeable future I wonder whether we do more than mildly bicker, but as of today that's all we do. You were conceived in love. If I know nothing else, that I know.

I read the first part to her in Munich, the first few pages, she said it was perfect. You probably disagree. Oh well… Time to stop in a minute, we'll maybe watch a film and then go to sleep after. Thanks for listening again.

Night has fallen in Rome, the cat is approaching, waiting for her little brother or sister. As we all are. She leaps agilely onto the sofa, nimble and dainty as ever. Your Ma is making me a cup of tea. Thank god, or whoever, for her, and for you, in my life. If you don't hear from me before, I'll see you Tuesday, little one. Bye bye.

Three

Yesterday we saw you. You waved at us. Kind of.

Five fingers on one hand, moving up and down, more like a cat scratching its face than a wave, actually. There *are* two arms and two legs too. Thank you for yesterday. And a heartbeat, a solitary thump thump in your miniscule chest. Your Ma was crying buckets onto her hospital gown. My mouth was open, my chin was almost touching my knees, gob-smacked, amazed, filled with wonder, incredulity, and thankfulness. We've got three little pictures of you now in the drawer next to our bed, and they seem more precious to me right now than thirty Mona Lisas.

Today you are the size of a lime, roughly. We think you were conceived at the start of November, which means you will be a summer baby, born at the end of July or the beginning of August. We'll have to wait. Today it seems very, very real and wonderful. This morning, writing these lines, I am sat at our dining table, while our friends Daniela and Kellen sleep in the next room. I'll have to get ready to go to work soon. Your Ma is already at her work. We've told lots of people about you already (via phone calls, Skype calls, and messages), and I'd tell every man, woman and child on the whole blue planet if I could. I'll tell my students and colleagues at the school about you too, and maybe show them a picture of you while I do. My friend Aiden said it looks like you are on the moon, I told him we'd name you Neil or Buzz. Don't worry, I'm only joking. We've still got the boy's name pretty sorted. The girl's name? Not sure yet, that might take a bit more of me and your Ma banging our heads together.

Let me tell you about yesterday. I finished working at four o'clock and raced to the Termini train station nearby to get the metro to Circo Massimo. As I usually do, I got there way too early, forty minutes before your Ma was due to pick me up in the car. It was just starting to rain, sprinkles of nasty drops dropping slowly, or at least it seemed to me. I huddled into a little café-bar and sat and drank a coffee, while some terrible music was being played on the television. I counted the minutes until she'd pick me up and take me to you, or at least the doctor who would let us see you. I must have drunk the scorching coffee in one or two gulps before I leapt out of the chair and did a power-walk up to the corner of the road. Your Ma was running a bit late. Time ticked, I'm sure of it, but it didn't feel like it, sitting on a damp wall, waiting in the ever-increasing rain. She came, finally, we kissed. "Hello, how are you?" And then ... Traffic, traffic, traffic. Rome is a beautiful city, and now even more so since it is the city of your conception. But it's busy and dirty and chaotic sometimes. It was probably only ten minutes in that car to the doctor's, but it felt like a lifetime. Finally got there, parked, find a place to pay for parking. Okay. Ring the bell for the reception. Ring, ring. Open door and walk up the stairs, holding hands, I hope, I think.
"Buona sera"
"Buona sera"
And then switch to dear old Inglese, the Queen's English. Fill in a form, name, date, address, numbers, words, a whirl of information. Thank you, please take a seat, okay, yes, thank you thank you. Our first sight of the doctor in the hallway; tall, grey, German, friendly, efficient. Yes, yes, we're going to see him. No, no. He's talking to another couple, a nervous African lady and her partner.

"But this is our appointment time!", I feel like screaming at him. We go into the busy waiting room, where... we wait. We wait. For thirty to forty minutes, probably. A short time? No, not then. Not that day.

We saw the African lady come out, a little happier perhaps. His long strides take him to us. He pronounced Colbourne a little strangely. We followed him, or rather he said: "Third door on the left", and we entered first. A desk, two chairs, a bed, and a scanner. My heart jumped, maybe we *would* see you.

This is what I remember: A babble of words mainly and your Ma in an ill-fitting hospital gown. Lots of questions from us. Short answers sometimes and long ones at others. We asked our questions (previously noted meticulously in a new blue notebook). Can I do sports? Yes, but not kick-boxing, he said without a smile. Skiing? Yes, no problem, please do. Your Ma wants to go to Colombia in March or May (you'd be there too). She asked, he frowned, the lines on his grey head angrily intertwining. No, he said, but I'm no expert, he said. "Oh great" I didn't say. To be continued, we say now.
"Would you like to see your baby?"
"Yes, yes, yes, god yes, a billion and four times yes", I didn't say.

And there you were, the baby on the moon, a heartbeat on a tiny TV, the size of a lime, half head/half body. Barely two minutes to enjoy your moment on TV. "Yes, yes, yes", he said. "All looking okay". "Oh good, good", we said. Tears dampened the gown. I muttered and mumbled and tried to form at least one semi-coherent sentence. Failed. Ask me now, today, for those pictures he printed, please. One is of your head and arms, lurching forward, as if crawling out of the picture. One is better, one arm near your face, the waving one I think, but no legs. The best one I look at now (phone next to paper). You're leaning back, relaxed. Right arm small and pulled back, left arm close to chin. You can see the body and two legs, too, pulled up. It reminds me of a sun-bather. Waiting for the cocktail hour.

And this is the photo we show. To Oma Petra in the car straight after. She can barely breathe, torrents of tears run down. She's ill now, but on that phone, she seemed without a care in the world.
"Du bist schwanger?!" she said over and over.
And then we drove on, to pick up our friends. To rush home. To set up my little computer. Your grandparents in England gradually flickered onto the screen. Small talk until the bomb was dropped. Nanny Pauline thought we'd got another cat I think. Granddad Malcolm blinked, dumb-founded. Questions and answers, we answered what we could. Tears and tears and smiles as wide as heaven. A hasty bye-bye, an email sent with the photo. "Bye bye, see you soon." And out we went again, into the cold, dark, wet night, as giddily happy as it seems possible to be. Excitement times twenty, tripled and taken and put on our frozen faces. It's on there now, too.

A pizza, a dinner, pasta, etc. Home, more people told: Granddad Roland, Uncle David.
"Whaaaaat?!" he said.

Same as your Ma when I asked her to marry me in Marrakesh.

My friends: Robin, Gaz, Asten, Aiden, Mo, etc. Ding, ding, ding went the messages, one after another. This is the effect you have/had on people. Smiles, kisses, splendid tears of hope and happiness.

I could write forever, but I must go. Shower, clothes, tram, bus, walk to work. I'll tell everyone, I'll tell the world.

"We are pregnant. And this is him or her."

Tschüß, Ciao, Bye bye, Toodle pip. Speak soon.

Four

It's been a strange day. More questions than answers. That kind of day. I feel like right now I could write a billion words, or maybe I'll finish at the end of this sentence. What is pushing me to push this pen across the page, to accumulate letters, words, and sentences?

The rain is quietly pitter-pattering, it has been all day. How do I talk to you right now and tell you about this day, this moment, this white piece of paper with black byro words, the green table cloth it lies on, the table it in turn lies on? The apartment, this kitchen or dining area or whatever it is I am in? Why tell you about this one room when I should be telling you about this world it is in? Let alone the country, which the longer I live here seems to make less sense somehow. Do I tell you about trying to find another pen? I've tried three but only one works. The words have gone from black to blue. Are you reading this now, or is it being read to you? My mind drifts. I think of Ernest Hemingway's: "One true sentence after another." Too simplistic. Back to black again, a quick shuffle into the bedroom to get another another another pen, my work pen, thin and plastic. Now I think of work tomorrow, only six lessons. Who knows who will be there opposite me? Faintly comprehending, no doubt. I feel lazy today, tonight. A day off work today and now baulking at the mere idea of six hours tomorrow... Lazy. Or 'pigro' as they say here. Mere details. I should instead tell you about the shape of the moon tonight, but you've never seen it before, how the clouds gathered earlier over

Piazza Venezia. How I almost bumped into people, as I gazed absent-mindedly at them. I could tell you about all the music I listened to on my MP3 player, which your Ma bought me one Valentine's day. We spent it apart, as I recall, it came in the post to your Grandparents house, where I was living at the time. I've hoped since that day that we would never spend another one apart. That moment filled me with a bittersweet longing that is hard to explain, or even fathom. She was in the Philippines, I was in England. I remember pressing the mouse button to the red icon to end the call, after several goodbyes, and then... A strange emptiness, the love flooding, famished and forming all at the same time. I wonder if you have found that love yet, or indeed, if you ever will. That sweet, but occasionally bitter-sweet, tangible aura surrounding you. Oh, let this old man talk to you about love, son or daughter, right now. Films and music are fine but can never be completely real. Real life is so much more immediate, but the tears do take longer to dry.

The fact I'm talking to a foetus via writing in these pages...

Welcome to week twelve, little one. Your hands are clasping, your toes are wiggling, and you, officially, are the size of a plum. Which reminds me, I need to buy a plum ASAP. Ask me now for the photos of a raspberry, a strawberry and a lime (your previous sizes). The lime is still in a make-shift fruit bowl, what we'll do with that, I don't know. Next week, a lemon, I'm guessing, but I was wrong last week, so you never know, huh?

How is your life now, former little one? Happy and healthy, I do hope so? And still we don't know the gender of you, our little one. I'm racking my brains daily, trying to put together in my mind, an identikit picture of you. I see... Dark hair, that's a given, I'd say. If you're blonde or ginger, well... And your skin colour will be fairly

Mediterranean/tanned looking, I'd think; Quarter Iranian that you are, mixed with your Ma's tangled Palestinian roots. By the way, we still haven't figured out how Palestinian you are exactly. Or you will be. What is the right tense there? Find an English teacher and ask him or her, will you? This one is useless tonight. Right now I have no preference on the gender question and maybe for a short while longer, I'll let my imagination gallop on a little more, farther on down the unknowable track.

Boy or girl, do you stare at the sky as I do? Like a simpleton trying to pluck a difficult answer out of thin air. Forever grasping. Do you look at your hair in the mirror too much like I do? Do you feel self-conscious in art galleries, as I did today? All the security guards with their eyes on me (or at least, that was how it seemed). Do you twitch your nose and eyes when you are tired? Do you even go to art galleries? What do you like? What don't you like, for that matter? Who are your friends? Who is your favourite Grandparent? Don't tell me. Who do you love? Who do you hate? Who annoys you? I hope you won't be angry or sad or miserable too often. I hope you won't be humourless, or cruel, or mean to animals. It's all possible at this stage. Every parent (with half of a sane mind) hopes for the best, but who expects the worst? I mean, are you in prison right now? Are you even talking to me or your Ma? Maybe you bullied, maybe you were bullied. Maybe all of your teachers loved/love you, or maybe you're one of those kids who the teachers talk about when they're drinking coffee in the staffroom?
'What about that bloody Colbourne kid, huh? Jeez, what's up with him/her? What kind of parents must he/she have?'
But I doubt it somehow, I reckon me and your Ma together almost make a normal person, and I reckon too

that you'll be just fine. No, I take that back. I reckon, really really reckon that you're going to be fantastic and fabulous times fifty-five thousand and three. You had a nice little wave at only eleven weeks. It's got to be a good sign.

There are some pretty orange flowers (I don't know the name of them, sorry) in front of me and a postcard to the left. It's a painting of Narcissus, looking at himself just before he fell in. The painter was Caravaggio, painted sometime between 1597 and 1599. Your Ma told a friend of ours, Nina, that I'm in love with him. Maybe. It's not easy to be in love with a murderous painter who died around 400 and something years ago, but I suppose we manage it just fine. I saw the painting 'in the flesh' today at Galleria Barberini. As the story goes, his egotism, his narcissism, doomed him, intent as he was, on staring at his beautiful reflection in the water. I like the painting so much, he looks carefully, concentrating and gazing longingly at his own face. As we all do. Like I said, me and the mirror are no strangers. A quick hand through the hair, a pat-down of a shirt, a re-alignment of one thing or another. Who can fail to see oneself? It's inevitable. But where we all go wrong (from the popes to the princes to the presidents to the paupers to the police to the Poles and to the Pakistanis) is thinking too much only of us. Only of us. Oh, let this (by now) older man impart one thing today. It's this: Think, think, think, carefully and truthfully, honestly, abundantly – of others. Yeah, yeah, I hear you say (or think, or swear under your breath) who's that joker (or worse...) to tell me this? He's no super-duper saint or son either (in my mind, right now, you talk and write as I do, with a predilection for using the same first letter of a word). But it's the only favour I ask: Try to be nice. And hey, if when writing all this, I can't impart or *attempt* to impart a little advice (I almost wrote wisdom...), what kind of father would I be, huh?

I'm still touching your Ma's belly every night, by the way. And whispering:
"We love you".
She'll be feeling 'tremors' soon, the little shakes before the kicking to come. I can't wait. Still, you remain three pictures and a thousand dreams to us. Maybe a thousand plans too. It's possible that you'll have already been to six or seven countries by the time you are born. Granted, the view is a little samey and you can't stretch your legs much, but technically you're travelling too. Right, so: Italy, Germany and Britain done, and to come: Croatia, Bosnia, Colombia. Oh, and the Vatican too. Croatia for Easter, with a quick trip to Bosnia, and before that, Colombia in March and then May (maybe). Not a bad little journey, huh? And no flights for *you* to pay for. Or passport control. Or those silly, fiddly fold-away tables on the planes. This, in turn, makes me wonder what nationality you are/will be. Let's just say European for now, okay?

Life is but a dream, know that for sure, and one day should follow another. Life will go on after us, and it went on before us. All of these questions will be answered, so, if you're tall or short, thin or fat, gay or straight, two heads or just the traditional one, two arms or three (in which case, you'll have a bright future as a juggler), sporty or musical or whatever you'll be: Ciao, Arrivederci, good night, sleep tight. Gute Nacht. Etc.

PS. When your Grandma Pauline was little, her parents (your great-grandparents, sadly no longer with us) would sing her a good-night song. The title is 'Little One', which, funnily enough, is how I titled the email I sent to them when I sent them the best photo of the three taken at your first scan. They, in turn, sang it to me, and I in turn again, intend to sing it to you (they, I'm sure, will sing it to you too, so you may actually be sick of the bloody song by now...). Now in 2018, as I look through the lyrics to 'Little One', another set of lyrics for a different song come up, and I can't remember the words properly. But your grandparents actually have a recording on an old LP. Here is the second favour I will ask today/tonight (here it's 8:34pm as I write, your Ma is out and I'm at home with the cat): Ask them to hear the song properly right now. God forgive me, I've not always been a perfect son, as I'm sure it's impossible for anyone to be (even you), but if you do this now, Nanny Pauline and Granddad Malcolm will be the happiest pair of people in the whole world. And hey, you may even get an upgrade on your upcoming birthday or Christmas present. Don't ever say I don't think of you.

Okay. Final good night: Good night, sleep tight, don't let the bed-bugs bite.

Five

I am sitting on the balcony. In winter. And yes, it is cold. The cat, slim little Pepper, is rubbing herself against my left leg, maybe in an unheard plea for food, or maybe she's just happy for the company. Why am I outside now on a chilly day, dressed in a winter coat and wearing garish bright-red trainers? I'll tell you. Today, as on most days, I have been thinking about writing and writers. Today, I am not at work and my to-do list is minimal. So, rather than do, I have thought, and very little else. It seems to me that some people are thinkers and others are doers. Your Ma, I think, is the latter and I am the former. Incidentally, back in England, in a city called Wolverhampton, I was playing football once and I accidentally fell and broke my thumb. Now it is aching as I write. Maybe a lighter pen will ease my pain? Wait there. Hold on. Okay.

I'm back, having returned with my trusty work-pen. With this I mark and correct and make notes about each student, and now I write to my child. My child. Last night, as I do every night, while I was saying goodnight and talking to you (via your Ma's belly), I finished with, as I always do.
"And we love you".
Same procedure as every night. But then I added.
"Our child".
This one word (child), is, maybe, the first time we or I have referred to you as this. Previously, you've been; little one, or baby, or strawberry, raspberry, plum, lime, or

lemon (am I missing a fruit there?). It felt strange and strangely wonderful. I repeat it in my head, those previously unfathomable words, slowly becoming comprehensible to me, and us.
"Our child. Our child. Our child".
I say it quietly to myself. This week I have told a few students about our news. About you. Yet you remain somehow myth-like, like a rare sighting of a mythical creature. Talked about, but only seen once. Thousands of words have been spread about you, yet you remain unspoilt, perfect, somehow, in your naïve unknowingness.

Good news spreads and reproduces, gives joy. So often, I have had cynicism and stoicism in my being, as I have written in the past. Bitter-sweet poems or stories with sad endings, a novel with a false feeling driving it on. How can I do this now? The cat is on my lap and your Ma will return home soon, bringing with her, you, in her belly, and although the skies are darkening outside now in old Monteverde, my hopes are soaring upwards, with the noisy seagulls, that, along with the other birds, fly off, somewhere somewhere. Meanwhile my friends in England text me, arranging to come here, ding ding ding goes my phone, various messages springing from my home to Rome.

It's getting colder. Still, I sit and scribble on. On past holidays, I have always been inspired to write. The unfamiliar surroundings spurring me on. I think of various apartments and hotels in Spain, Turkey, Cyprus and numerous other countries, always with the same foreground. My left-hand gripping the pen (as I do, somewhat frenetically), churning out lines, with a beer or a glass of wine next to me. Write, sip, write more, sip more. What makes me want to try to create something out of nothing? To fill a page. Money? No. Fame? No. To impress? Perhaps. Today, there is no booze as I remain booze-free since August of last year. While the spring and the summer were marvellous and certainly memorable, the sun put a glass in my hand too often and I wearied (and faltered). So, now I refrain. Coca-Cola, tea and coffee will suffice, and, surely can be enough. Twenty-odd years of the bottle may not be a distant memory just yet, but the need is slipping, it claws away, not as tight as its previous hold. A good thing becomes a bad thing in excess, but we live and we learn, or at least, hope to. As you will too, I have no doubt.

Colombia, here we come. It did seem a little doubtful at times, but right now, barring another dose of the bad-news-blues, we're all set. The three of us. Bogota in March, it has a nice ring to it, I think. Your Ma will work, and I will write, wander and wonder. On Friday (tomorrow in fact, this week has flown by), you and your Ma will go to Austria and Germany, to ski, where you may feel the snow in your undeveloped bones (and you may hear the voice of your Ma's friend, Ina). I will be here in Italia with your big sister, Pepper, trying to avoid *her* claws and occasionally feeling her tiny teeth in my old wrinkled hands. Don't worry, it's only for two nights, the vast majority of me will be there with you, only my body, I will leave in Rome, for work and words. That vast majority, as I hope you know, will always be with you and your Ma (those things, like, say, for example, my heart, my soul).

I'm getting sentimental and trying to hide it with thinly veiled 'humour', whilst also knowing that cynicism is not my friend. I can't help it, I was born and raised with it, I suppose. The 'English disease', they used to call it. Not being able to show your feelings. Not like the Italians.

Their feelings are everywhere. Veritably bursting out all over the place. I'm a Northern European, sadly. But perhaps the Persian in me will one day come to the fore, and I'll hug and kiss everyone, tell them all my whole story within an hour, all the time. While giving them dates, obviously.

I couldn't write for a minute there as Pepper was on my lap. We're still outside, huddling together for warmth. She's sitting opposite me now, nestling the wheel of your Ma's bicycle, which is also outside with us. And there she goes, trotting nonchalantly into the apartment.

My hands look older than they should, my face a little younger
My legs have travelled, one foot in front of the other
My eyes have seen many things, but continue to roam
While I continue on, left foot and right foot, on
My finger is sore with the writing
My stomach grateful for its fullness
The left eye is lower than the right
The right testicle has left
The left one is fine, thank you very much
My hair is thinning and showing some grey
And I don't always do the wise thing
But I heard I have a soul
And I'm sure there's a heart.

Arrivederci little one, until we speak again, until we greet one another, one fine day to come, know that you are 'Our Child'.

Six

I'm inside, in the relative warmth, sat at the dining table again, and I think of you, little one. How do you do? What do you know? Where will you go? I think of you, child.

Today or tomorrow, you are (or will be), unofficially, the same size as a peach. One hour ago, I tried to buy one at the market. The man looked at me like I had three heads and eighteen arms, he said something or other about the sun or the summer. 'Something or other' because my Italian is only a tiny spot above my Mongolian or my Moldovan. Perhaps we'll have to take a picture again, like we did with the plum. Long story…

I'm not at work again. It's a Monday and I have every other Monday off work, to compensate for working every Saturday, I suppose. Mondays are on my own and Saturdays are at work. Meaning me and your Ma are apart for half of the day, which I don't like. Increasingly, work is becoming for me, well, work. The lack of organization, the complaining teachers (of which, of course, I am one), the unpredictability. It's a place that keeps me away from your Ma too, perhaps worst of all. It's terrible really, but I'm only half of a person when she's away, waiting, on hiatus, you could say. She left Friday morning, to go to Austria, to see her friend, and to ski, and returned Sunday night. So, in fact, there was only one measly day (Saturday), in which I didn't see her. One day.

Is it more manly of me or less manly, to admit that to myself? But, admit it, I have to. I promised you I'd tell you the truth, little one. If your Father can't, who will? And your Father, I am, it's inescapable, that fact, and I'll always have it, no matter the future. So, thank you again.

I'm not (too) naïve, I know what a strange uncertain place this world is, complicated by its humans. We're a frightening bunch, there's no doubt. Prone to a thousand things and only a third of them any good. I can no more protect you from this world, I feel, than I can stop the cat from walking on the table, as she is, as I write now. Of course, I will do everything in my (limited) power to protect you, to help you, to guide you, if you'll let me. Even now, having just returned from a mere walk to the supermarket, a 'lady' shouted at me because I walked in front of her car. I apologized immediately, but it wasn't enough. A volley of strangled syllables, she unleashed at me. Perhaps its better if I don't understand, sometimes. This country confuses me; the noise, the dust, the sheer velocity of its people. So different from my own, my British Isle. And I thought the Germans were different...

Today I write, tomorrow I will work, tonight I will cook for your Ma. Earlier, I bought some flowers for her. Sad little specimens they are, crowded and malnourished in the vase. Oh dear. The odd florist guy said "Ten euros", I said "What?!", he said "Four", I said "Okay, then". Always trying to outdo one another we are, us humans, us tragically flawed specimens, pushed against each other, like the falling flowers, in the vase I glimpse at now. Yes, it's a strange day I do think, quiet and foreboding, or so it seems.

Your Nan and Grandad have been in Spain this last week, returning yesterday, I think. Your Ma had a nice time in

Austria. But I dread the thought of a week without her, in May, when she will go to Colombia alone (apart from you, sorry). And, in fact, right now, my bosses are umm-ing and ahh-ing (as we say in Brum) about my holiday-leave in March, also to Colombia. How can they separate a man from his wife and child, you might wonder? Easy. Self-interest, pure and simple. Or, rather, self interest wrapped up in a veil of friendliness, just like the weirdo who wrapped your Ma's flowers. I wish you strength in this world, little one. Male or female, girl or boy. I wish you light for the dark times. Silly old Dad is rambling on now, huh? But how quickly we become old and how slowly we become wise. If at all.

I met your Ma from Fiumicino airport last night. Yesterday, I didn't do too much. A long walk in the park, and reading, and reading some more. While you were warm inside, your Ma was on the ski slopes of the Alps, whooshing down mountains. She's just now starting to show her baby-belly. Our secret has slowly and gradually been revealing itself these past few weeks. More people have been told 'the news', more well-wishers. More of everything. "Boy or girl?", they all say. "Dunno", we reply. "Doesn't matter", I mumble, more to myself than to anyone else.

Shave, shower, feed the cat, lock the door, down the stairs, open door, shut door, down the road, green man, cross the road, walk, walk, walk, tram, train, airport, terminal 3, find arrivals, wait, wait, wait.

And then there she was. One big blue bag dragging along the floor. Me, dressed in a suit. Your Ma, surprised look on her face because of this, jumped. She jumped, I exhaled, I caught her, we kissed, we hugged. I think there may have been some sweet nothings mumbled into one-another's ears. I put her down and we went home, with you.

Why does a person love another, truly? Why do we do it? Their look, their smell? Their eyes, their ears, their hands? Or their everything? Their heart, their soul, the rather peculiar way in which they brush their teeth? The way they hold your hand? The way they hold you closer and closer until...

God knows, or maybe, even he doesn't, why we're complete with that other half. And then two make a third, and then... And then... I don't know. Lots of words, I suppose. Spoken mainly. Right and wrong.

One day in late July or early August (we don't know yet), we will return home again, with another person. For real, for real. In a car, I suppose, you will be, blinking and bashful, confused by the summer sounds and smells. And then we will open the car doors and we will scoop you up from your special chair. And carry you, up, up, up, two flights of stairs. One of us will take out his or her keys and open the door. And they will have to do the strange hissing 'Ksss! Ksss!' noise, so that Pepper the beast will not attempt her little party trick of running up the stairs outside the door. And then... And then?

I swear, I don't know. It will begin. For real, for real. Maybe you'll be crying, maybe you'll be sleeping, maybe you'll be hungry, maybe smiling, maybe going crappy in your nappy. Questions and uncertainty. This is what the smart-ass, wise-guy, know-everything websites and books don't tell you. What then? Oh, they can tell you how to change a nappy blind-folded, while only using one small toe on your left foot. And they can inform (at length) for pages and pages about what you should and shouldn't do and when you should or shouldn't do it. But they don't tell you what next, when the door is closed, when all the bags have been put down. What then? Your Ma will be tired, no doubt about that. Shall we let her sleep? Okay, it's a deal. And then? I'll need a cup of tea, I think. Okay? Okay. And then, while the kettle boils, while the steam is rising, when the tea-bag is in the mug and the milk is ready to pour... Then and only then, I will carefully pick you up, up, up, tightly and truly. I will look deeply into your eyes and say-

"This is the world".

You may seem a little disconcerted at this point, so I will pull you close to my chest. And then I will say, as softly as I can muster, and over and over...

"I love you".

Until that fine day... Bis später.

Seven

Good morning little one. You are currently having your first experience of horse-riding, albeit, via the warmth of being inside your Ma's belly. Don't worry, the horse and your Ma will do the hard work, you've just got to keep on doing what you've been doing. Last night was a nice night. At one point, your Ma said to me "Happy hiids, we are".

In our silly little couple-language. Usually every Saturday, I go to work for four to six hours, teaching. Usually children, but often groups of adults too. They're a mixed bunch, for sure. From seven to sixty-seven. Lately, while you've been circling my mind, I wonder which of these children you might resemble, if not in looks, but where it counts, in your character. Like the hyperactive (nine years old today) L, equal parts crazy, tired, lovable, and maybe a tad annoying too. Or like eight years old, I. A more grown-up child you could not imagine meeting. Extremely delightful, but it's also a little unusual (unnerving even) to talk to an eight-year-old who talks like a fifty-eight-year-old. Or poor little frightened E, or her frighteningly self-assured sister B. Or ten years old, C, adopted and African, guile-less and genuine. Or even nine years old L, who told the receptionist that I am an excellent teacher. I was a little touched when she told me this, but I did also think this: 'What nine-year-old boy talks like this, seriously?'.

Like ultra-smart N? Shy and sweet T? Cocky and clever A? A right little madam like G? Which one will you be like? Components of all, or maybe none of the above? We shall see. Now, I suppose, as you read this, or it is being read to you, you are a teenager, or perhaps older. That's another kettle of fish. To imagine you now is mind-bending enough for me, the same size as a navel-orange that you are this week. To imagine you sitting opposite me, aged 7-12, speaking English, like the students do, even more imagination is needed. But as a teenager? Wrestling thoughts of exams, spots, the opposite sex, and dreams previously unseen, slowly slotting into place. Well, that's too much for me, too much for my meagre imagination. Right now, imagining as I am, as I do, I see you in the smooth woollen little suit that your Ma bought for you, wiggling and wriggling ten fingers and ten toes, and I smile.

So your Ma is on the clippity-clop horsey while I write this morning. No work, only horse-chores (cleaning the cat crap out and washing dishes etc), eating, drinking hot tea and coffee, thinking about chocolate biscuits (I just ate three, don't tell anyone). Wondering and wondering. She will return in about an hour and a half and then we will set off, the four of us. One male (British, big nose, lovely hair), one female (German, big eyes and funny little ears), another female (also German, feline, pisses where she feels like it). Plus, another: You (male or female, baby, unborn) will all set off in your Ma's little blue car to Umbria, to Todi in Perugia. Off we'll go, a little road trip.

The land of your conception is Italy. But you I think will not really be Italian, more like 'made in Italy'. Raised, I don't know where. Schooled, I don't know where. You'll be a baby of the world, comprising of four nationalities yourself, having been to several countries before even being born, and then... The future is unwritten. Exciting and unknown, incredible and incomprehensible. But don't worry, you're in (relatively) safe hands...

On Tuesday, we will see you again. I've never been too keen on going to see a doctor, but, for you, I count the days. In the past, for me at least, it's all been about coughing in waiting rooms, cold-eyed receptionists, finding the right room, waiting to be seated, explaining awkward and uncomfortable things, and then... clothes off. 'Does this hurt?' 'Does it hurt here?' 'Do you have a history in the family of so and so or such and such...?'. 'Errr, no, I don't think so...'. A frown. Words scribbled, scruffy, almost Arabic with their unfathomable characters. No one writes like a doctor writes. They can heal almost any ailment, but, ask them to write a simple comprehensible word or two, and they'll write like a dyslexic simian with broken fingers. And then? And then you go to the chemist to get something, or, if you're unlucky, the speech will start with something along the lines of 'I'm sorry to have to tell you this' or 'Well, unfortunately...'. Deep breaths and sharp intakes of oxygen. Bad news is delivered badly, always with fumbled words, kind meanings and meaningful kindness. And received with dumb-founded fumblings and fumbling dumbness.

But as I said, a trip to the quacks with you, and for you, is a different matter. I'll gallop up the stairs like a champion prize-horse, clippity-clop will go my heels on the concrete. I'll wait patiently for the receptionist (who now seems to, maybe even, be smiling a little, and even if there is a cold-eyed approach, I'll fail to see it, such will my optimised optimism and good cheer burn through the pessimism and hum-drum...). I'll gladly wait again, in the waiting room, maybe rifle through the delightful old magazines, whilst holding hands with your Ma, tightly. And then the call will come.

'Colbourne!' or maybe 'Mrs Colbourne!'.

I'll leap out of my seat and trot to the doc. 'Hello'. 'Hello'. 'Hello there'. Pleasantries and more pleasantries. It's nice to be nice. 'Thanks for waiting' 'Yes, no problem at all' 'How are you today?' 'Very good, thank you' 'Please take a seat' 'Yes, thank you'. And then...

Maybe on Tuesday, we'll see you again. Maybe on Tuesday, you'll wave again. Maybe on Tuesday, he'll tell us this... Boy or girl... July or August.... That all is well.

Okay then, let's have a look....

A heartbeat, two arms, two legs, one baby... You you you on a black and white screen. You you you, not yet a teen. You you you, barely a baby. You you you, definitely, not maybe.

Who knows? No-one knows. Not me, little orange. Not your Pa and not your Ma. Not Grandma, not Grandpa. Not your uncle and not your cousin. No one knows. The wind will blow which way it wants.

It's 11.09. Your Ma is on a horse, the cat is on a sofa, I am on a chair, in an apartment in Italy. You are with your Ma, inside, warm and happy. Stay there, little one, until the time is right. And then, and only then, come out to play. We're going to have so much fun.

Eight

We saw you again yesterday morning. How much you have grown. It is still hard for me to fathom, even now, as I glance at your latest photo. The pictures were taken less than a minute apart by the doctor and so they are practically identical. You seem to be lying upside down on a ceiling. Your head, disproportionate to your body, is leaning forward, left hand tucked in, so only a bent hand is visible, the right arm is up, in a wave. The legs seem to have an unreal alien-like quality, the left is bent also, the knee is clearly visible, and the right is pulled back. Your Ma suggested before the appointment that we could or should film the video footage. I was against the idea at the time because I didn't want to be holding my phone and looking at that, instead of you, on the screen. Now I feel it may have been a good idea. Two ghostly images are all we have of you, so far, all I can hold on to. I can't wait to look you in the eyes, to hold your hands, to hold you, to see you, for real, for real, for real, my child, our child.

I am off work again and writing at the table. It's a cold but sunny day and I should be outside really, enjoying my freedom, away from work. But so much is being downloaded into my teeny-tiny brain right now that perhaps it is better if I empty a little onto these pages. Today, so far, I have flipped between reading a book about ancient Rome, doing chores around the apartment, and oddly mooching around the place, restless, wandering aimlessly.

July the 30th, the 30th of July, a Tuesday. A Leo you are likely to be, and if the 30th is correct, then it's a Tuesday, and as your Grandmother reminded me yesterday, Tuesday's child is full of grace. She is also writing to you, in a journal (as she describes it). Yes, you've become quite the muse. Impressive, I think, for an unborn person, I think you'd agree. And a person you are now, with hair and fingernails, eyelashes even. Your Ma said it felt strange watching the video screen, of you, forgetting almost, she said, that you were in her. So clever now, the technology we have, I think, but to you reading now, all of the technology here in 2019 will be obsolete, replaced long ago, dusty on the scrap-heap.

We weren't able yesterday to find out the gender. Boy or girl, girl or boy, you're keeping it a secret. The doctor said that next time (a whole four weeks from yesterday. Too long. Far too long), probably, we could find out. I wondered at the time, how he could be so casual and obtuse about it all. But now, I suppose, I do realize that while this is our first baby on his screen, for him, the number must be in the hundreds, if not thousands. I tell people that the sex doesn't matter. "Boy or girl, either way, I'm happy", I say. It's half a lie, I suppose, I admit to you now. I want to know. ASAP. As soon as is humanly possible. Old doctor N and his gangly ways have a job to do. But I am bursting. You are on my mind so much, little one, and my love is flabbergasting, and not paid for by the hour.

It's week seventeen now, we had to jump a week, so me saying "Goodnight, little avocado", only lasted two nights, snuggling my face onto your Ma's expanding white belly. As of this morning, not officially, but close enough, you are the same size as a pomegranate. Very Persian of you, thank you. Well, I'm sorry that I can't introduce you to my Persian familia familiars this year, but, never mind, I suppose they're out there somewhere, in Leamington, in Iran, or even down the road, here in Rome, for all I know. Perhaps one day...

Today, again, you are with your Ma, at the United Nations World Food Programme, just lying around, while she works, or maybe right now, she's eating lunch, or even laying down the foundations for our next big move. Vienna, Panama City, Kampala, Bangkok, Amman, who knows. Knock three times for Vienna, two times for Panama, one time for Kampala, four times... Well, you get the idea. Where do you fancy spending your first year or two? Oh, or Beirut too, that's a possibility as well. Sorry, I forgot that one. Maybe your first five or six months will be a real whistle-stop tour of travels if we get our way. Your passport will be full up by the time you're out of nappies... Two weeks in Rome, two in Germany, two in England, two in Japan, four in France, four in Greece or Cyprus (or how does autumn in Spain sound?). And then, off we'll go again, pick up Pepper from Nan Petra and then off we'll skedaddle, cat toilet in tow, suitcases full to bursting. No worries, no pressures, you don't even have to bother going to the toilet... What a life.

Tonight, I'll cook for me and your Ma, she's ever-so tired lately, carrying around, not just you, but her funny little ears too. Oh well. Olivia Emily, Emily Olivia, Emilie-something. Something Yasmin, Yasmin something. Samuel something, something Samuel. Samuel from your Great-Grandfather and Emily from your Great-Grandmother. Yasmin is Persian, Emily is from the Latin 'Aemilia' (which means to excel, apparently). Olivia, which was first used in 'Twelfth Night'. And the agreed upon, almost set in stone, Samuel, is Hebrew (name of God or God has heard). So, there you go, a lesson from your favourite teacher. Or possibly least favourite teacher? Who knows, after all this meandering? Maybe today, you are named after one of these choices, maybe not.

What should I tell you of the world you'll be falling into? Bloodied and confused, crying, and as innocent as anything gone before it. What should I tell you? Well...

Water is wet
Wet isn't always water
Water's in the sea, but so is salt
Salt's on your chips
Which sits next to your fish.
Fish are in the sea too.
Japanese people eat lots of fish.
And there are lots of them too.
And they're in Asia, which is big.
Bigger than Europe
Which is where we are today, okay.
Tomorrow, I don't know.
More importantly, importantly,
You are you
And I am me
And Ma is Ma
And the cat is crazy
And that's all you need to know today.
Tomorrow will come tomorrow.
So, we'll look at that
Tomorrow.
Together.
Cheerio for now, little melangrano.

Nine

Little one, I'm sorry, I haven't written to you for twelve whole days. My bad, I apologize, bad Daddy, silly old man, mucho stupido Signor Colbourno, as the Italians don't say. Have you been waiting, little one? Have you been listening each night, me talking, and saying goodnight to you? Through the layers of skin, flesh, blood, walls and walls until the words touch your tiny new ears. Ears that have only recently moved down to their proper place, where they will stay, from now on. I'll try and make up for it, with every syllable now. It's my day off, and it's a sunny but windy day in old Rome. Your Ma is at work, Pepper is chasing around an old ping-pong ball, making a lot of noise, and I'm sipping hot coffee at the kitchen table. What can I see? White flowers, two little plastic penguins, a notebook with two llamas on the cover, the previous pages, some blank pages ready and waiting, and a bible. Not mine. The outside door is open to the balcony, a pleasant and gentle breeze blows through. The sink is filled with dishes, the washing is drying, my phone is being charged, my belly is full, life is being lived. Two old ladies walk by, I can hear them, yap-yapping in their (mostly unknown to me) Italian. Loud, expressive, I'll bet their hands are going around, in circles, up and down, 'ten to the dozen' as we say back home. I've thought about that this morning. I've presumed, foolishly, that English will be your first language, unfair to your Ma and her parents, perhaps. But who knows, maybe you'll prefer German, or whatever tongue is being spoken in the country of your upbringing? Spanish, French, Italian, Arabic even?

As you know, I have some competition in this writing malarkey (will you even know what this last word means? Will you ask me the meaning, like your Ma does, sometimes? Will you even read this sentence? Or is it all merely vanity and rambling, to be written and never read?), I asked your Granny Pauline (it's strange for me to write that now, or even think it) what she was writing about, last night during our skype call, she wouldn't tell me. "It's a secret", she said, with a wink or two. Not even Grandad Malcolm knows, at the moment. And, actually, vice-versa. She doesn't know either, that I'm regularly writing to you too. You were a secret for a little while, and your gender shall, or should be, a secret too, at least for a little while. You were mine and your Ma's secret, and now this writing will be too, for the foreseeable future at least.

She's also made you a blanket, little mango (for that is what, roughly, you are the same size as this week). You're going to be nicely kitted out. Old things and new things, like them and you.
Okay, let's get back to the lesson about this place, this world, this solar system, this universe of ours.

Red is for passion, romance, and anger. Blue
Is for the sky, the sea, and you
If you're a boy, it's what you'll wear, it seems
Green is for the grass, nature, and trees
Orange is for oranges, orangutans, penguin noses
Oh, and red is also for strawberries and roses
Yellow for the sun, daffodils, sunflowers
Grey is for the pavement and the sky when it showers
Pink is pretty, for a pig with a tail
And what you might wear, if you're a female

White is for clouds, paper, and sheep
Sheep go 'Baaa!', and to count when you sleep
Brown is wood, trees, and poo
Black is what you see when you can't see through
Oh, and I suppose there's purple, which doesn't rhyme at all
Okay, those are some colours, you are very small
So we'll save the rest until you're a bit more tall.

Lately, I've been teaching lots of kids who are complete beginners. Teaching them numbers, months, the days of the week, emotions, and occupations etc. These are the things you'll learn too, in at least two languages. You're a foetus right now, barely six inches big, with tiny fingers, tiny toes, sleepy eyes, and a funny little nose. It's a lot of pressure getting ready to come into this world. And it's not always easy here. People kill people, sometimes, for lots of different reasons, the seasons come and the seasons go. There is sun and wind and rain and snow. Sometimes it's warm and sometimes it's cold. You're unborn now, but one day you'll be old.

As I suppose you've noticed by now, our little mango, I do like writing to you, like this, jabbering and jabbering away to my heart's content. I do mean well. I always will. What you see and what you'll be, are to be decided, all surprises. One day, once upon a time, I told my Ma that I wanted to be good at one thing, just one thing, to bring smiles, salaries, and happiness to me, me, me. I was a teenager, I think. I insisted, persisted on moaning in my poor Ma's ear, "I'm not good at anything". I don't remember the response, to my shame, but the blame I was laying, was all at my feet. Feeling sorry for oneself is for boring people, it's tedious, but, of course, we all do it, especially me, sometimes. This is my confession: I doubt it's my profession. My lessons in their little ears, well, what they hear is rarely heard. And it's not sport, or cooking (definitely not), or dancing (although someone once said I was an excellent dancer. Yes, she was a little drunk, but even so…). Or singing or kissing or kayaking or whatever. But I do hope, pray, five times a day and to whoever will listen, that I'll try my damnedest to be great at this one thing: being a Daddy.

Oh, this life is so strange. So big, so incomprehensible, never sensible, always strange. You can never rearrange all the pieces of the jigsaw, you just, sort of, sort through it, trying to be patient, hoping for a clue.

Through your life, you'll stumble past
Friends that pass and family who'll last
But people will come and bother you so
Much, you'll feel ever so low
Times will come when you're blue as can be
It'll be impossible to see the wood through the tree
But time heals wounds, old people say
When they're old and wise and a little grey
And they nod when you talk, knowing this game
They've played it too, different, yet the same

So, yes, I do have hope that I'll be a good Papa, as patient as my Ma was with me, that night, quite a few moons ago.

Your Ma wasn't well last night. She's okay now though, hopefully. She came home feeling dizzy and disoriented. We started cooking, she was so confused, putting flour in the fridge. We were rushing, foolishly, cooking, eating, all at top-speed. It was a migraine. She had a tablet and then went to bed. Pepper, with her perfect timing, decided to piss all over the bed sheets. Bless her today, but yesterday, well, I cursed her yesterday, spraying her stream and giving me hassle, too much hustle and bustle.

At night too, when all your poor Ma wanted was deep dark sleep. We did sleep eventually. And it was a whole new world again this morning, as it always is. Sun and nice tea-bags dangling in our cups. Cereals, and a smile or three. "Good morning, my love, how are you?". The sky was blue, and I said "I love you". And kissed you both, and away we went. Just a little bickering, a little cuddle, a little kiss, the day, undeniably, was new. It still is, in its own way.

So many visitors coming. So many plans. Planes and trains and cars and ferries. Old people, coming to see young. Vice-versa, versa-vice. It's week nineteen. Twenty-one to go. Slow. Slow.

Life has been lived for centuries in this old town. You are growing. We are waiting for the curtain to rise...

Ten

Spring is really here now. A lot is happening. My parents and uncle left yesterday morning after four days, here in Rome. Because, lately, I've only been seeing them three or four times a year, I notice and feel all of our aging, in increasingly stronger cycles, or so it seems. The time before was at Christmas, for just a few days, in Sutton Coldfield, at their/my home. Aging is a terrible thing, I feel like I will very soon be on the cusp of it, the slope downhill, or rather, not uphill. In two years, I will be forty.

There are, I hope, many great years ahead of me, but as I watch your Ma's belly grow and see each week what you are as big as (this week, bizarrely, a banana), I remind myself that time is precious, and that the clock is ticking, and it always will be. Again, I am at home with the cat (currently playing with, and clawing at, a paper bag on the floor), writing to you, thinking of you and your Ma, always and endlessly.

Next week, we will all go to Colombia (except the cat who will stay here with your Oma Petra). Usually, before travelling to a new place, I like to research the city, or country, or destination.

Pause. Fresh thought.
It was my intention and aim at the start of this little project, to tell you the real story of these days and months before your imminent birth. What was really happening,

the truth, and all of the seemingly pointless and tiny little occurrences. While I have been writing these past few moments, I have smelt a rather strange smell, an odd lingering odour, wafting in the breeze, and it was only two minutes ago that I realized what the smell was. It was coming from the flower vase. Realizing that they probably needed new water, I put my pen down, in order to change it. The smell viciously emanating from the emptied vase was quite putrid, similar to the pungent nastiness always coming from the fish market, over the road from us, at San Giovanni Di Dio.
So, I washed it all out with soap and boiling hot water, all the while holding the flowers, like an Olympic athlete on the podium, awkward and a little gormless-looking.

Pause. Stop. Fresh thought. My mind is again galivanting. I bought a banana earlier. With the intention of taking a picture of it, with two plastic penguins... Did I really just write that sentence? Why? Because, each week, as I may have mentioned before, I take two pictures, one with the fruit-of the-week and your Ma, and one with the two plastic penguins, which have (sort of) become like our little mascots.

And again, while I was writing about the flowers and their smelly water and vase, my miniscule mind wandered off. It seemed incredibly important to take the picture. And Pepper joined in too. I wonder if you think of me, now, as strange, reading or hearing these pages? As I hope you do (or hope you are). So, the picture has been taken and the image has been sent to your Ma on WhatsApp. I've been waiting for a response from her to my previous message, about the weather in Bogota in March. Alas, no response, as yet. And anyway, she's working, and she's not a Colombian weather girl, so why am I bothering? But then again, the messages haven't been sent, which seems unusual. They have only one grey tick next to them.

And yes, these are the small things I think about as I write to you today. At 14.12 on Wednesday the 6th of March 2019. These small things, these private jokes and details. Another intention of mine was to tell you about the world you will be entering, in approximately, twenty weeks from now. What is happening?

Well, BBC news on my phone tells me that:
North Korea is rebuilding a rocket site.
Thousands of people are stranded at Kenyan airports.
The football team Real Madrid, is at the end of an era.
And the weather in London is 13 degrees centigrade.
Then it moves onto the daft unimportant things. But bear in mind that millions of people will look at this today. And this is what they will see, what they will read about, and what they will discover:
Why are avocadoes and kale so popular?
Will fashion firms stop burning clothes?
A Chilean paraglider and his hawk.
Oh, you'd be surprised at what passes for news these days.

Wars are raging, people are starving, people are dying of thirst, people are enslaved. Living, dying, thriving, and struggling. The rich are getting Botox and the poor are making do. This is the world, this is life. Babies are being made, being born, walking, talking, screaming, sleeping, puking, crapping. People are making people, killing people, burying, cremating, mourning, sailing, swimming, soldiering, selling, sending SMS's, scoffing salad or sitting at bus stops, train stops, tram stops. Planes depart, planes land. Planes go up and down all day long, from Switzerland to Swaziland, Scotland to Samoa,

Spain to San Marino. Seamlessly, the skies fill up with planes, and they fly, fly, fly, miraculously, the planes float around the multitudes of clouds, soundlessly, speeding through invisible air. Except in Kenya, I suppose.

Bicycling, belching, burping, becoming, burning, beginning, babbling, bagging groceries, bailing prisoners, bamboozling the simple, banning immigrants, banishing, baptizing, bargaining, barricading, bashing, batting in baseball, begging, behaving, bellowing in small apartments, bereaving, betraying, bettering themselves, bidding, blaming, bleating, and bleeding. We all bleed. Red as roses, and scars always show.

Yes, this is world, or, at least, the b's. The bees are buzzing, I imagine.

Pause, Bogota.
Bogota is the capital of Colombia, and beyond that, I know very little. Well, except that it is very high up, and well, that's about it. Perhaps, I should do some research.

The smell is back. Why? Why? Time to throw out the old white ones and keep the pretty purple ones. Hold on a minute... okay, I'm back.
Bogota. But, pause. Pause.

I'll tell you one very important thing right now and I hope you don't blush. Okay, now, let us all be adults, at least for a couple of minutes. Okay? Okay, then. It's about escalators. Metal steps, up and down. Me and your Ma like kissing on them (I hope I'm not being presumptuous about this). A lot. Almost every time, even when we're with other people. So much so, that if we don't, I start to wonder if she's upset with me. Yes, every couple has 'things', and that, I suppose, is one of ours. If your cheeks are slightly red, then, I apologize. Or, maybe, you already know about this by now? Don't ask me why. It's a tradition, I guess. Just be glad, beautiful blushing child of mine, that your parents do (or did) this.

A lot of this is guess-work, right? I'm talking, essentially, to a foetus here. Give me a break.

One day I'll tell you how me and your Ma met. That day was the fourteenth of November 2015. A special day, in many ways.
But back to escalators, yes, when I'm with your Ma, I just like a little kiss or three. I plead, I beg, I implore, I ask nicely, I request formally, I require, certainly, I inquire, prudently, I suggest, obviously. I even demand, occasionally. "Just a little kiss, pleeeeease". And I try to do my best puppy face. Which rarely works.

But when I'm on my own, and this is a bit strange and very particular, so bear with me… I, kind of, write in my head, which does seem slightly mad, yes. To put it another way, I think about writing, but not only that, I write, without pen and paper. I, just, kind of, do it in my head. Almost every time I'm on an escalator, on my own. Up or down. And, I swear that, it's the best 'writing' I've ever done. But, yes, it remains, technically, unwritten, left in the recesses of forgotten memory. All the best writing I've done, left on escalators. With my hand on the rubber thing and my feet on the narrow steps. I've often thought that, if I had a Dictaphone, and could, somehow, record these things, it could work. Then, I could, actually, write these things on paper. These thoughts. As it is, I don't, and they remain in the unseen air, like dust blown away. The wind pushing it towards oblivion.

Now I think of parks, and Pepper, who doesn't seem well, sneezing and shuffling around, poor little bugger. Your Ma still hasn't responded. But back to 'How I met your Mother', it's a television show, it ran for nine series, had five main characters, great music, and...

But the story of how I met your Ma will have to wait a while. Suffice to say, it's a long one and I've told it about a billion times to people, always via mouth words, not paper words. But I'll save it for you, little one.

I've written a lot, but you're worth every word
You're worth the pens, the ink, the stink
Of these flowers, these hours
Go by. Go by
You're worth the paper, worth the trees
Worth the sun and worth the breeze
Worth waiting for, worth dying for
Living for, losing sleep, losing it all for
The years go by, go by
And this world is crazy, but I'll try, I'll try
And when the day comes, as soon as it must
We'll take you up
On the escalator, with us.

Arrivederci, little banana, boy or girl. Kiss, kiss.

Eleven

Big things are happening, little one. Little hiiid. Yes, indeed, Sir or Madam, girl or boy, lady or gentleman, child of mine, of ours. Today, tomorrow, and every day, big things are going on. Today is my 'special day', and also the birthday of your Grandad Malcolm. The line, reaching from him, to you, as your Grandfather, is a short, but slightly different one, to what is considered the norm, I feel sometimes, due to the reason of this here, 'special day'. And last night, I did actually say to your Ma, that soon (for soon it shall be), for the first time in my life, I will have a family member with the same blood as me. My features? My idiosyncrasies too, perhaps? Hopefully my patience, but hopefully not my nose. Thankfully, my parents, yes too, for if you will not share their blood, you will share your youth, or a part of your youth with them, and that must be more important. It is a slightly unusual situation, for sure. I grew up with parents who resembled their parents. I guess, you won't resemble my parents, but, who knows. A small thing, and a big thing, maybe.

But big things, big things... Tomorrow, we'll see you for the third time. Your heart, your brain, even. On that little screen at the Doctor's office, that I've come to anticipate so much. We'll wait for him to ramble a little and then your Ma will lie on the strange bed-like table and put up her feet, and then, one thing, and then another, and then, there you are. Tomorrow, tomorrow, who knows what you'll bring. Boy or girl is the big question on my mind right now, but instead, it should really be health. Your health is your wealth, the one most important thing, for all else comes after that, little foetus. Are you healthy? Big or small? Ten toes, I hope? Four limbs a-quivering, a-moving, a-shaking and a-baking in Ma's oven? Let's hope so. Everyone has health issues in their lives and you, my child, will be no exception. Let's hope, let's hope, that they will be only sniffles, a little trapped wind, a little, only, of anything. I hope, we hope. But come what may, tomorrow and tomorrow's tomorrow in ten, twelve, twenty years time, we'll look out for you, look after you. This, I swear. This, I can promise. After weighing up all the things that can happen, go wrong, or go right, the sex of a child must be a tiny issue, a minute functional distraction from 'the big Q' that always finds its way into my head. This one, this Q: Is he or she alright in there?

Big things, big things. Grandad Malcolm is sixty-nine. Still dancing, still smooching, still enjoying life, still pretty healthy Insha Allah/God willing/touch wood (whatever will work, really). And Oma Petra is coming this week with her pal to look after the complex cat, the ferocious feline, little pissing Pepper. And your Ma is having an interview today for a possible job in Vienna. I'm guessing now, and I'll know more later (so, I could be wrong), but I'm predicting you won't be growing up in Austria (probably). Or Panama either, that's not happening. It's only fair to tell you. Uganda, Jordan, Thailand, Lebanon (maybe I'm missing one here) are all still in play. Yes, yes, I should start Spanish, or dial up my Deutsch, or even attempt Arabic. But definitely the Deutsch. I can't have you speaking the German lingo, and me not understanding. No way, no way. Do you fancy France in autumn, or Kyoto in fall, or an English breeze blowing through your thin hair September/October time? A chilly Bavarian November? A Tokyo time when the leaves fall slow? The world is our oyster, little one. So much to see, so much to do. God grant me a full lifetime, so I can skip along all the shores of the world. With you. Until they call my number, and the boatman wants his money. Let him wait. Yes, let us make him wait.

Big things. Colombia. Bogota is calling in three-days-time. Your Ma is all packed up (and trust me, that's miraculous), and soon I shall be too. Shirts and shoes, socks and shaving foam, books and boxer shorts, pens and paper, so I can talk to my progeny. The tickets are printed, the passports are primed. We've been immunised against every insect under the sun, so let them
all come, and let us not be afraid. Let us not panic about Zica viruses, muggings, knives, guns and guts churning from bad burritos. Let us skip, let us cartwheel, let us fall, and bounce back up, with a cheeky grin and barely a scratch. Let us see our friends Alejandra and Maria-Jose. Let us smile, let us sing, let us hold hands in that funny way we do. Let the sun shine on and on, let words tumble, even fumbled out of our grin-lined lips, let our souls spring up like tulips, let love wibble and wobble. Let there be hugs, let there be kisses. Oh yes, let there be kisses. Oh, and don't let me get lost. You know what I'm like...

Big things. Rocking and reaching the tops of the trees. Tomorrow, I'll tell my boss "Bye-bye, but in the summer there's gonna be a little one coming and he or she needs time and attention, baths and burping, so sorry, buddy, but I'm offski. Toodle-pip." Yes, that is what I should have written earlier, when I did my official resignation letter...

Big things. Wrestling doubts, head-locking fears, rubbing knuckles against the head of hardship. Humour abounds in these glorious days, silliness surpasses sadness. At least in this destination, this table, this chair, right now.

What else? Books are waiting to be read, films waiting to be seen, eager students line the streets all over the world, and need people like me, ready to grab them and grammar-them, pronounce the 'th' in this, that, there, those. Yes, these are the days I hoped for when I was stuck and strapped in tight, counting the minutes of the slow days in warehouse purgatory. These are the days I wanted, worked for, worried about, even, if they would come at all. These are the days and the ghosts have all gone. These are the minutes where all the mind is free, free to eat an ice-cream or two, free to dance with the cat, free to sit in the midday sun, free to open up a book and put up one's feet, free to finish the chocolate biscuits, free to write and think and fucking do whatever I feel like doing. Bye-bye guillotine, literal and metaphorical. Bye-bye forklift. Bye-bye E, bye-bye S, bye-bye G, etcetera, etcetera. Arrivederci moaning managers, Auf wiedersehen nightshifts and nuisances. Adios to the cold and the cunning ones. Oh yes, these *are* the days, my friend. I'm happy today. And my hair looks lovely. Just lovely...

Oh yes, I know, frowns will return, maybe today, maybe tomorrow, whenever, I don't know. But pessimism can park itself a little further away today. It's my special day and I'm going to be a Daddy.

Big things, baby, big things.

P.S: I'm sorry about the swearword earlier. I'll try not to let it happen again.

Twelve

The spark is in me now, to write, nice and hot. The light is burning. Old-school hotel room, back upstairs, turn the key or flash the card to walk in and then pen and paper and away we go. A flashback, throwback, to the days of taking pens from bookies, or pencils from Argos stores, then maybe buying a newspaper, and scribbling a poem, or lines for a future poem, in the margins, or in the light-blue sky of an advertisement, anywhere or everywhere. It was glorious, even in the darkest days, the flame for writing was never defeated. And I feel it now. Beautiful and strong. Thanks to you. My daughter. Thank you. Gracias.

Yes, your secret is out now, little one. No more hiding behind the bladder. No more boy or girl conundrums, no blue or pink. We know now, we found out on Tuesday morning in Rome. It's Friday afternoon in Bogota here now, but maybe more on that later. We're going to have a little girl, a daughter, another female to add to our little travelling circus. The Doctor, old Herr N told us. Or, actually, kind of deduced it. By not being able to find any testicles. Not very scientific, to say the least, I'd say. But, he said, certain, he said, girl, and I wouldn't change it, or you, for the whole world on a platter. Don't worry, we won't cover you in pink, from head to toe (although others may try…). If you want sports instead of Cindy, that's fine. Boxing or ballet, either, or both, is cool with me, these days. Your Ma said, when hearing the news: "Hello, Emily". For this is now your most likely name, maybe with Salome' as a middle name. Like your Ma and Pa, you'll have five letters. I don't know why that seems worth mentioning. Hey, by now, you know that I'm a little weird, right? I can't write too much now as time is a little limited, and paper also, by the way. I had to scrounge five sheets off the lady on reception. I wanted ten, but meekly asked for "six or so". I wonder how many I could have gotten out of her before she would have said that I was taking the piss (in Spanish, whatever that is)? Ten? Twenty? Fifty? Oh well, your Ma will be coming back here to meet me soonish. Luckily, she has only had to do four or five hours today, after yesterday's mammoth trip. Four hours from Rome to Madrid and then a hefty twelve and a bit from Madrid to Colombia.

So, welcome to Bogota, little one. Baby girl. We think you like it already. This morning, me and your Ma were struggling to sleep, tossing and turning after all the travelling, our minds restless, no doubt. We put our hands on her ever-increasing bump, and what did we feel? You, probably. It was like a pulse, or a heartbeat. It's hard to describe. Not kicks yet, we think. More like 'flutterings', which is how 'The Pregnancy Book' describes them. Yes, it was a moment for us. The three of us. We smiled those kinds of smiles, which are the best ones of all, giddy and simple, unabashed and untamed, our silly little happy smiles, which, I like to think, we only share with each other. Our baby was moving. You were kicking, or punching, or dancing perhaps. Either way, thank you again, little one. Little girl, little Emily. How I love to write this name now, Emily, Emily, Emily, knowing as I do, just what it means.

This is (another) strange interlude or pause in proceedings... but anyway, here I go... There was a gap, just, of maybe five minutes, between writing the word 'means' in the above paragraph, and writing the word 'This' as the first word of this one. What does this mean? Well, to you, and probably 99% of the known world, it means absolutely nothing. But this is something I've thought about, on a fairly regular basis, since my school days. We see the words piled up into sentences, but as a reader, this is all we see. We don't see the gaps, or the pauses, or the breaks, or the nipping to the loo, or putting the kettle on. This has always, kind of, fascinated me. And I don't know why. In other words, the stopping of the writing is invisible and unknowable. We see only what they show us. In this little project of mine, one of the aims was to tell you about life as it really is, or was. It's not a fiction at all, or even literature, as such. It's just me, talking with a pen in hand, to you. With gaps.

Another pause. This time, for only three minutes. The first pause was a nice pause, your Ma returning from her work today, and telling me a little about it. Then I returned to the page and the pen, while she turned on her laptop to send an e-mail. This second pause was less happy. She must have seen it on the news. Forty-two people killed in a terror attack at a mosque, in New Zealand. Forty-two people, at least, as sadly, the numbers do tend to go up in these kinds of things. Some sort of far-right white supremacist group went into the Friday prayers and killed these people. Why? To me, to any sane minded person, this should be seen as senseless. But to use this one vague word to describe it as such, doesn't even begin to start. Evil. One of my reactions was that this 'sort of thing' doesn't happen, normally, in New Zealand. In Iraq, for example, it is depressingly frequent. But in 'our homes' too, in Britain and Germany, it has been known. Nowhere is safe. All over the world, it happens, all over this strange world. We become used to (terribly, we do) the chaos and mayhem of destruction, far too easily, if it is 'one of those countries'. We shouldn't. Every death in this manner is a stain, a permanent mark, on our human race. Yes, it is tough, to tell you about a tragedy like this, especially having started out these pages with tales of good news and happy moments, but, like I said, this is the world you will come into. All of it's joys, all if it's sadness.

All of its joys. Like waking up in a new country, kissing your Ma, feeling our child move, an amazing breakfast, then walking hand-in-hand, chattering aimlessly, meandering these streets. And then…

All of its sadness. A fight broke out (more a few punches thrown, in fact, than a level-sided fight). I saw it fleetingly, slowed down and strange, like these thing are perceived, travelling from eye to brain. Strange. At first, I thought they were playing or just boys-being-boys (silly boys…). But then a fist, the handsome boy on the floor, another young man standing over him (or maybe crouching over him?), two or three more punches. A little blood, a broken nose, and the assailant (for that is what he was/he is) striding off, down the busy street.

A pause. The maid knocked. "No gracias", I said. She said something, your clever Ma translated. Now your Ma is lying on the bed. I'm writing again.

And why tell you about the incident in the street? Because life is not a vase of roses with the thorns removed, life is not caramel-covered toffee and fudge with dollops of ice cream on top. Life is not always what we want it to be. But it can be. Don't forget that. It would be remiss of me to paint a pretty picture of this planet and the people populating it, it would be negligent, even.

I hope, today, that the boy's nose heals, and his pride too, even quicker. I hope the attacker feels some remorse, or at least, not pride, about what he did. I hope that bloodied boy on the floor can forgive him. I hope the families of the victims in New Zealand can mourn, recover, eventually find some peace. I hope. We all hope, we have to. Its uncertainty makes this world incredible, for good and for bad. But it does require a little hope, now and then.

The last page, from the lady on reception, is nearly full. Rest is calling me. And then Bogota can come again. You, just keep on growing, and lay all your worries on my shoulders, I suppose they're broad enough. Daughter of mine. Emily, Emily, Emily. It's a wonderful world too, of course, and we'll do our best to protect you.

Your Ma is dropping off to sleep, I think... I'll say Adios now. Until the next time, dream sweet dreams inside, until you are outside.

Thirteen

Hello little girl, our daughter. This week, you are the same size as an endive, or a radicchio, if we're talking Italiano here. Week twenty-one of waiting in Mama's comfy oven. Keep growing, moving, breathing, floating, waiting, until the end of July, or the beginning of August. Keep on keeping on, tiny Emily. This weekend, we had about sixty thousand potential names thrown at us, suggestions suggested. But we three know the truth, the reality, don't we, little one?

Away on another continent, South America. Here, away from Italians, and Italian and Rome, and home. Away here, with a multitude of foods, peoples, races combined, to make a fine country. I like this country, this continent, this city of opposites and arepas. Funny, how I look more Colombian than my blonde-haired or ginger-haired or blue-eyed white-skinned hombres back home. I look more Spanish than Sutton Coldfield's average, somehow. Apart from the red-neck little sunburn. Not very Persian of me. Fail.

Blame the horses. Yesterday was your second time (albeit, in your Ma, not on a hossy). Trotting, lightly galloping, always aware of the precious cargo inside. My horse seemed obstinate and strong-willed, Whisky was her name. We went on through the mountains, four horses and five people. Our poor Colombian friend, A, shrieking and squealing all the way, bless her, her first time on a 'horse'. How her poor face dropped when your

Ma told her that it was actually a mule (kind of a half donkey/half horse hybrid). Me, your Ma, and her daughter, MJ, plus the guide, holding onto A's 'horse', a patient man, seemingly used to quietening and calming first time slightly hysterical ladies. Up and down we went, taking pictures. You sat, or crouched, curious, no doubt, in the belly. Your Ma in her pretty little newly-bought hat, clever teenaged MJ, wise beyond her fourteen or so years, and her poor shrieking (but cheerful when on her own two feet) Mother, and me up-front, wondering just where the hell we were going, not knowing that old Whisky knew exactly where to go, and what to do. It's hard for an old city boy like me to trust a horse, I suppose.

Yes, it was a good weekend, and it's a shame you didn't see the rolling hills, the old town, the clean hotel, the lively locals, the scrumptious food, the cobbles in the square and almost everywhere, the bright light-gold in the church, the life, and the alive. The majestic horses, calm around the storm of humans, gracefully and agilely showing us people just how it's done.

But so long in the chugging rental car, to that lovely old place, bumping and thumping in our temporary transport. Many miles there and back. And your poor Ma, our patient (or trying to be...) driver, with stomach cramps, sunburn (her poor little pink hands), tired eyes, tired feet, tired everything. Poor thing. Back to Bogota and our new room. Yes, it was a fine weekend and life is good, I do think, for our new little clan.

One more memory from yesterday. On the way back, we stopped off at an important national area, commemorating this year, two hundred years since the battle that supposedly (I am told) pushed back the Spaniards into their boats, back to nosey old invade-y Europe. 1819 it was. Lacking much knowledge, I let my imagination canter a little, muskets, horses perhaps, swords, I suppose. Blood and death on green hills. A country becoming free and colonialism taking a well-deserved blow to its metaphorical nose. But the history point will not stick with me. No. This will. We stopped the car to get out, stretch our legs, and see the site, the plaque on the wall, this important time and place in our friend's country's history. But the ladies were tired and many steps had already been stepped, so it seemed as if we would take a picture and then get back in the car, and set off back to the big city. Until the spirit of your Great-Grandfather (Leonard Hipkiss Senior) must have jolted me, and I suggested running a race with a confused-looking MJ, down to the bottom of the steep hill, to take a picture of the plaque, and so on.

Let me rewind the time back to 1989, or so. I was about eight or nine, so my Grandfather would have been in his sixties. Running down an equally steep embankment, carrying a football. Only wanting to play football with his Grandson? Yes, perhaps. Eventually, his mind sadly eroded with the Alzheimers, that would eventually take his final years into murky waters. But I swear he never lost his spirit. For me, he will always be a man who had a twinkle in his eye, always ready with something to make us smile, and forever with the comedians quick-witted zest for life. So, fast-forward thirty years, and it was he I thought of, as I sprinted down the hill, charging, in my mind, like a Colombian freedom-fighter, towards the cannons. Free willed. An adult is a person with adult responsibilities. And has adult things to do in an adult manner. But yesterday, I raced , with a young girl down a hill, and then cart-wheeled at the bottom of it. And then charged back up again. God can help me, forgive me, or forget me, and I'll leave it up to him what he chooses, but he can't take away my silliness, daftness, and playfulness like a demented kid. The love of this life. And I won't forget in a hurry, charging and sprinting (like a big mad silly old bastard) down that emerald hill. And when back up, I pondered to your Ma, whether or not, when you are fourteen too, I will be able to repeat the feat. I'll be fifty-two, she'll be forty-five. Let's do it. Let's be silly. Even if I have to hop on one old damaged foot. Let's be silly, stupid, strange. Sanity is for the strong amongst us, so let us be weak on weekends, sometimes. And the ghost of my Granddad will smile at us. Gloriously.

I bought a whole ream of paper earlier. It may break my back when I carry it back home to Roma, but until then, it sits pretty, serving as a kind of mascot, my goal too. An Everest to climb with words. Can I write five-hundred pages? Can I complete this lengthy task? I'm no Dostoyevsky, Tolstoy or Turgenev, no Russian genius, scratching masterpieces from a cold harsh landscape. I'm no Camus, Sartre or Proust, pontificating the mysteries of life as we know it. I'm not J.K. Rowling or Stephen King either. Perhaps, no one will read these words, apart from, maybe you, and that's not a given. So, this big Colombian packet of paper, well, it's for me, and your Ma, maybe. And maybe you. Maybe, baby, I'll bore you to tears, maybe this will gather dust. And rust. Maybe, maybe, the dreams I have will wither and decay. Or, maybe, little baby, it's all to play for, all to fight for, all to jump, reach, grasp and go for. Sod the cannons. We all have our battles. May yours all be victorious, or at least, well-fought. May mine stay in my eyes, when the time comes, quietly.

I pulled the plastic beads, the blind went up. The sun came in and has lit up the dust, the desk, and the paper. I see trees, taxis, total light bouncing off buildings, old and new. A new looking white car goes around the corner, tentatively. A woman, with a back-pack slung over her right shoulder, saunters on down the street. Shadows play and dance on this street. I hear the pen pushing out words, I hear a cough in the next room, I hear rustling, people rummaging around. I feel the sun on my burn, the watch on my wrist, the pen in my left hand, pushing the skin, making its mark. I feel a little hungry, a little tired, quite quite happy. I smell the sun on my skin, I smell the arepas' packaging in the bin. And I see, hear, feel and smell that there is a time coming, that babies are growing, that there are people here, there, and everywhere, going somewhere.

I look deeply into my reflection in the window. Who is that man? Wasn't there a boy there, only yesterday? It's blurry, un-formed, I can't see my face, only my arms and legs, what I've done.
And if I can't see you yet, only on a screen
I can dream, I can wish, I can hope.
And wait.
Wait.

Fourteen

The rain is dropping, it won't stop. The rain is falling, it always does, and always will. Not much is certain. But the rain is. And it's always annoying and wet.

So, I sit here now in this little hotel room in my T-shirt (which could do with a wash to be honest) and my blue boxer shorts (which have red-lensed sunglasses on them, as all great boxer shorts should have). And bitty grey socks. My clothes are drying, I'm not a weirdo, or at least, not 'that' kind of weirdo.

Quiet day, a slightly strange kind of day. I went out earlier for an hour or two and got fabulously soaked to the bone, soaked to the skin. I walked the streets and had to point at things (like food, mainly) to get them. A weird rice and egg ball and an odd stringy meaty thingy thing. And a chocolate bar, and even when I pointed at that and said the name of it, the guy asked me a tonne of questions, a machine gun patter, 'da da da da da da', of Spanish, and I felt like a silly English fool, muchos stupidos. One chocolate bar. Maybe the questions were about if it was the only thing I was going to order? Or something along those lines. I don't know.

More foolishness. I got a little lost. Again. And was becoming more and more damp, like a squid in a shower. I kidded myself that it was 'only rain'. 'Hey, no problem, it's only water'. Then the real rain cascaded down onto my soft head, hoodie clinging to my melon-head. And that's when I gave up. I decided to wait for a taxi, but at least ten empty ones ignored me. Why? Finally, one stopped. I got in, told him the area and address. Another rat-a-tat-tat of Español. "Uh-huh, uh-huh", I agreed with him, dumb as a mule. Then he stopped and gestured for me to get out. Luckily, it was a spot I recognized, so I could walk back to the hotel. This refuge, this room, this desk, this chair. And now?

Yes, a little bit of a strange day. Is it even raining anymore? I see no drops, but the clouds look mean, threatening, nasty grey cotton-wool shapes, up there in the air. I should probably go out again, but I feel my race is ran, for today, at least. I wish you were with me now, little one. I could take you to a park, or a zoo, or a playground, or anywhere we could imagine. I could do something wonderful with you, I could pick you up, I could hold your chubby wee hand, left or right. Yes, I'm restless, it's unnerving. I could, equally, sprint ten miles, or, just go back to bed. I should go up the mountain. Or at least up the steps, outside the hotel.

So I'm writing, I'm revving up to something, I'm not reading to anyone what I've been writing to you. Maybe to your Ma, later though. I think it has stopped. Yet I'm compelled, now, to sit here, tap-tap-tappity-tapping the pen against the A4 paper. Unsure and overly-aware of this predicament, this gift and this curse.

I've made a note of all the things I want to tell you. But I won't right now, sorry, Emily. This morning, we felt you again, or was it last night? We let our imaginations run riot, especially me. But you're still the same size as an endive, a mere radicchio. It's easier to think of you as a small fruit or a vegetable, sometimes. Less responsibility that way. Buying clothes for you makes it realer, easier, looking in shops, for things, for you. Each item, I've lifted up, as if you were inside the clothes, and it wasn't just a lifeless piece of clothing. The 3 to 6 months things look huge, preposterously so. You will fit into these things in less than one year from now. But last week, you were barely a banana, only growing the same size as a mango the week before that. It's incredible. And I'm incredulous. Struck flipping dumb, by the near future. I carry on with life, even this escape from reality (as this Colombian adventure feels to me, right now) is fleeting, but also slow, unerring and unusual, but a prelude, somehow to the life-changing orchestral cacophony coming in just a few months.

I'm going to be a Daddy, I tell myself, in my mind. I'm going to have a daughter, with my wife, Sarah. The marriage thing is relatively new, too (together for forty months, and that's pretty new I'd say). A mere three and a bit years, I have known (and loved) your Ma. From meeting in Cambodia, that Siem Reap slow sunrise when I said goodbye to her. And then hello again in Hamburg, the day after boxing day 2015. Then Berlin, Paris, Prague, Amsterdam, Rome, Barcelona. Keep going, and that's just Europe. Include Lisbon, include Sicily, include Switzerland. Keep going, further afield. We've seen Morocco, the Philippines twice, hand-in-hand, cartwheeling and skipping, eating and breathing, together. New York was a whirl, Boston was behind us in a flash. There's more, there's more. And I'm not trying to remember here, I'm not showing-off, just telling you, and me, that since the 14th November 2015, life has been a great ride, a trip to tell about, a short journey, but a lifetime of memories. And it's only been forty months. And now here I am in Colombia, writing to our daughter. Our daughter. I love those two words.

I'll tell you now, little one, little dream, little miracle. We met in Siem Reap, lived in Berlin, got engaged in Marrakech, got married in Denmark, lived in Rome, conceived you in Rome. Where to next, little one? Now that you're a big part of the story, it's only fair that I ask you. Where should we go? Which sun? Which rainbow? Which star? Which table should I lean on, next? This planet, please. Just tell us, and we'll plan it.

Details, details... We're on the magic-carpet ride now, there's no stopping us. Once upon a time, I lived in a cold country, with another woman, did another job, and dreamed smaller dreams. Here's the thing though, here's a truth in all its incredible-ness, you're the one I've been waiting for, for a long time. How many young men want to have a daughter? Not many men, young ones especially, will stand up and say that, but I would have. And now I'm a not-so-young-man, when I glance into the mirror, but I am a lucky son-of-a-gun, a lucky little so-and-so. Be happy and then be happy again. I've returned to writing to myself, of course, but I suppose you already knew that, didn't you?

Life is making something out of me. Life is calling. Life wants me to grab it by the scruff of its neck, and scream something incredible in its ear. A life is coming, another one. Yours. And maybe now, the rain will stop. Maybe, baby, I will run up that mountain, fist-bump god, and say thanks, for her, and for her Ma, and for my Ma, and my Pa. You, me, us, everyone.

Let's go.

Fifteen

The truth is that you can't see much, at the moment, little one. Just yourself, blood, and the inside of your Ma. It's not much. But I suppose your eyes aren't as complex and advanced as they will be. Your Ma is in an office working, about a ten or fifteen minute walk from here (depending on who's walking, she's slowing down a bit, these past two weeks, carrying you). This morning, we woke, dressed, had breakfast together, downstairs in this hotel. Then I walked her to the office building, across the road. And now, I sit, again, at a desk. This is our third room in this hotel, we moved twice, because originally we didn't book the weekends here. It's Monday morning. I hear faint voices, outside. It's 11.41. I'm dressed only in a T-shirt and boxer shorts again, as I have only just awoken from a long sleep. The blinds are up, all four of them. The skies are cute, a gentle blue. The clouds surround the prettiness and have grey centres. This is what I can see, I, your Father. This room is overlooking a play area in a small park. Ten minutes ago, there must have been twenty to thirty people there, now I peer out, and see only one, a man, sat straight-up, on a bench. I peek at him through the window, through the bunches of trees.

Pause.
Your Ma just sent me a text message. She told me that her meeting with the Director went well, and suggests meeting at a café at 6.00.

Where did all the people go to in a hurry? I glance again at the lone figure on the bench. Maybe, actually, it's a woman. What is she looking at? What is she thinking? In England, and this has happened to me a lot of times, I'd say it's almost customary to talk to people at bus stops, when you sit next to them. I remember once, when I lived in the Castle Vale area of Birmingham, I was waiting for a bus, to take me into the city centre. An old lady sat next to me and started to make conversation. That expression 'making conversation' had never seemed more appropriate as then, as I struggled to construct a chat with that person. Luckily, the talk was mainly all about her, as I recall. The woman has gone, two boys are hanging on some railings now, they're dressed very brightly, a woman in sunglasses has emerged now, and another smaller boy has joined them, they are all sitting on the grass, near the bushes. Soon, the woman was telling me all about her family. Her deceased husband, her daughter, and so on. Then she told me, in a rather abstract way, like it was a very minor detail in the story, that her son had died. Not only that, but that he had killed himself. Not only that, but that he had hung himself, and she had found the body. I must admit that I was only half-listening to her, until that point. Until her arrival, I'm sure I would have been listening to my MP3 player, impatiently waiting for the bus to take me to bars, or shops, or wherever.

"Of course, guess who walked in on him. Huh? Me!"

"Oh, errm. I'm sorry"

What could I say? What would you have said? Why did she feel the need to tell me that, then, that very moment? The trees are so dense below that I can't see the ground, mostly. Only the two small paths of the playground and the building block across from here. The kids have gone, an over-weight man in a tight but smart shirt is walking slowly backwards and forwards. What's his game? That means 'What is he up to?'. It's a phrase I use very rarely, your Ma would never use it, my Ma would, and her Ma too, I think. Not my Grandmother Pem (or Emily), the one you are named after, my Ma's Ma, Connie, short for Constance. The man has gone, it's completely empty again. That bus-stop is just a one-minute walk away from what was once my Grandparent's house. In the past, back then, although a child is unaware of such things, or at least accurately aware, the area of Castle Vale had a reputation as a bad area, a bit rough, a bit dodgy. And, in fact, when I bought a house there, many years later, a friend of mine said he'd take me home, but only in a tank. But my Ma grew up there, some years, happily enough, with her sister and her brother, and her parents. I was talking to your Ma about the house the other day, about how it had a particular smell. A smell of cigarettes, but also, a kind of musty smell. It wasn't an unpleasant smell at all (as it must seem as I describe it here). The kitchen, which was on the left, after you walked in, through the brief hallway area, smelt slightly different, a bit fresher. I recall both smells so clearly now, it's like I'm back in that house again, a kid, waiting to be asked if he wants an ice-cream or a biscuit. The large living-room was to the right, and the garden behind that, which for some reason, I have no memory of being in. The steep stairs were in the middle. Up to two bedrooms and two small bathrooms, I think. My uncle's room, I remember well, as my cousin and I would stay there sometimes, overnight in sleeping bags (mine had a tag with a Native-American chief on it, wearing a blue and red head-dress). My Grandparent's room seemed off limits, and very tidy, when occasionally glimpsed. No reason to go in there.

I remember that sleeping bag very clearly, it always seemed a little difficult, in the middle of the night, to recollect that it wasn't a bed, it was a sleeping bag, on the floor. Feet entangled, and then a few kicks later, and pulling up the zip which had moved in the night. And then extreme comfort for just a minute or two, before blissfully dropping off to sleep again. The chief, inside, with me.

I'm leaning on an A4 sized book, now, as I write, the bottom inch of the page is becoming increasingly creased, as when I write, the page moves up and down, off the book, and my left forearm is squashing it. The book seems to be about, what back then, I would have described as, Indians, meaning Native Americans. A shame then, that I don't speak Spanish (or at least, nothing beyond a few numbers, hello, how are you, you're welcome, thank you, some food, some drinks, and 'no more'. 'No more or 'No mas' because of reading about a legendary boxing match between Roberto Duran and Ray Leonard. After so many rounds, the ultra-macho Panamanian Duran, had had enough of Leonards taunting and 'clowning', and he uttered the, by now, famous words, 'No mas', to the referee, to signal his will to stop the fight. Duran had won the first fight between the two, making his decision ever the more perplexing).

My uncle visited us recently in Rome for a few days. He is seventy-five now. He lent me a book once about those two boxers, plus the other two stand-outs in that great era for boxing. It may be the only book he has lent me. Few people have lent me books. Your Ma, my friend Gary (known to all and sundry as Gaz), my Ma, not many others. I have read books of others, of course, but not many, and very few have recommended them to me. Your Ma and my Ma have wide varieties in taste. My Dad, a little oddly, I always think, read the books of only one writer, the American thriller/horror writer, Dean Koontz. By now, I'm sure, he has read well over twenty-five books of his. Reading (or literature or whatever you want to call it) has always been immensely important to me (as has boxing, I suppose, to a far lesser degree). Yet many people 'in my circle' don't really read, or if they do, read books that are of limited interest to me. My aunt tends to read chick-lit, another friend reads sports books, almost exclusively, a rather odd ex-colleague of mine would occasionally lend me books about crime or prison. Another ex-colleague, a friend of mine (extrovert, loud, cunningly intelligent, a little aggravating sometimes...) lent me, not one but two, about East Germany, and a book solely about cocaine. I lent him one about the football world cup, I thought he'd enjoy it, and he may or may not have. I do know that he never returned it. I would love to know where that book is right now...

And this book I lean on looks interesting. Filled with grotesque pictures of torture and cannibalism, historic photos of indigenous people. But all in Spanish, a language I don't understand (your Ma would, that clever Ma of yours). As this city, this country has also been hard to fathom, at times. On Saturday, we went to a photo exhibition, about some of the very recent troubles of the country. The photos were mostly of grief, or at least, the ones that really stuck in my mind. A grieving mother, a distraught child, a Grandparent holding up a photo of their missing, innocent little Grandchild. I am not the right person to explain this conflict to you, I don't qualify. Suffice to say, many, many innocent people died. Young men, soldiering on order, killed, maimed, and raped, and in doing so, forever lost their own innocence, their own humanity. Boys, killing, mere boys, or barely men. If you had been a boy, we would not have bought you toy guns. A shame, a real shame then, that I couldn't understand the texts on the wall of the exhibition (although your Ma did provide some context), same as I don't understand this book, underneath this piece of paper.

There is a boy, swinging upside down, a man and his dog jog by, and then a moment later, gone, vanished. Empty.

It will be time to say goodbye to Colombia, tomorrow evening. Your Ma will return in less than two months from now. As will you. Before I came, I thought of cocaine, footballers, Gabriel Garcia Marquez (his book of short stories is currently confusing, and entertaining me), Shakira, and, well, not too many other things, to be honest. Shame on my ignorance. Just mere slips and snap-shots of a vast country. I should read more history books, huh?

And now, on the 25th March, another Monday morning, where the clouds now cover us, this hotel room, this country now, after eleven days of being here, am I any wiser? Debatable. But I'll take back memories. The chaotic centre, death in photos, Botero's fatties, food glorious food, our friends, the mountain, the cable car, walking up and down the city streets, taxi rides, kind people, loud people, crazy people, people in their element, their country, the parks, the wispy trees, the elevators, the escalators, the music, everywhere, and yes, this here hotel, this place, this country we came to, with you.

Now it's 12.56, and I'm still in my underwear. Three pairs of boxer shorts are drying in the bathroom. I didn't bring enough, so I had to wash what I had, in the sink, with hot water and kiwi-smelling shower gel. I'm quite a strange man, in many ways. Yesterday, your Ma finished her application for a job in Geneva. Who knows, maybe you'll grow up like a little Swiss girl? Whatever that means, I don't know.

Yesterday, we also went to church, together. Songs, a sermon, well meaning people, a jokey pastor (they are all jokey these days, probably an improvement, probably a good thing). And me and your Ma. Afterwards, we spoke of our impressions, she was quite content, overall.
I said that it was strange for me, as an atheist, to go to church, and I questioned, out loud, just why I had done it. I thought that my real reason, that, to be honest, it was more for the sake of her, than for me, so we could go together, was a little flaky, a little foolish, a little bit of a weak reason. I told her, we talked, she said that she appreciated me going with her. Perhaps, that's enough. She also said, that after listening to me reading these pages to her, sent from my head to your future ears, that she thought I was more agnostic than atheist. I don't know, I'd guess the latter, but if the former's cap fits, I'll wear it, for now.

Your Grandfather, Roland, once won some money. I don't know how much, the figure doesn't seem too important. Once, when speaking of faith and these kind of matters, your Ma told me that it helped or re-enforced his own, coming as the win did, in a difficult moment, financially and personally. I would compare these two events, his win and your birth, as miraculous happenings, but I can't, or at least, not yet. As his event helped him, 'my' event has not yet occurred. You are not yet born, not yet walking and talking, not breathing the outside air. When I was a child, and I asked for something, my Father would say "We'll see".

So, we'll see.

On Saturday, we bought you a dress, a beautiful thing
One day I hope to see you in it
One day soon

We will put you in it
Or it over you
We will zip it up, do it up, fit you in it
We will flatten down the creases
You'll have to grow a little
To fit in it
But, grow you will
There will be a photo
One day soon
You, in it
A little girl
Called Emily
In a dress from Colombia
One day
Soon.

Sixteen

Back in Rome, back to our sort of home. Back to writing at the table, with the door to the balcony open. Back to watching the cat, to see if she's pissing or not. Back to work, back to school, back to life, back to reality. Back to pizza and pasta and pupils and 'Grazie', not 'Gracias'. I haven't written to you for ten days, I apologize, daughter. The jetlag (if that's what it was) made your old Dad feel even older. Yesterday, I woke with a strange despondency, lurking inside me, unexplained and unwanted. Nevertheless, I went to work my six hours at the school. Italians, a Peruvian, a Moldovan, a Pole. The time went by, the hours passed. I am ready for a change now, ready to leave Rome, ready for the end of July or the beginning of August. Ready for you, little one. In my mind, it's a slow goodbye, a meandering last dance at the end of the night. The drinks, having been drained...

To us, now, you seem more real than ever before. Real in the pictures. Real in the baby-carrier we now have, in the wardrobe, ready and waiting for you. It fits well and does work (don't worry...), or at least it seemed to when we put the cat in there, nice and snug she was, our little 'test pilot'...

Real in the plans we have, the talks we have about you, real in the doctor who tells us about you, real in the midwife's house that you may be born in. I should tell you about that house, it's likely you will cry your first cry there, breathe your first breath, open your eyes, and see strangers. Among the strangers will be me and your Ma, so have no fear. Real in these pages for you, this is the ninety-third. Real in the faces of my parents, who will wait even longer than us, to see you. The fashionably late star, superstar celebrity. Real in all the words, in all the people, who say "Boy or girl?". But only we know, only we have that secret under lock and key, in this little family, just the four of us. This new international family. We'll tell them only with a slip of the tongue, only by mistake, only with an "Oops" after. I don't want to tell them. We created you, your Ma and Pa, Sarah and James, you're ours, we are yours. Real in my resignation letter to the school, real in your Ma's colleague's eyes and ears, when she tells them about you for the first time. Real in the new clothes your Ma needs now, hastily purchased when found, real in her expanding waist, expanding almost everything. You're so real.

Real in the research we do, looking for a bib, looking for a bed. A little bib and a little bed and a little everything, for you, all ready and real. Tiny person, hello. Tiny baby, how are you?

And real in my worries. My mind has its corridors where you crawl around. Are you okay in there?

Certainly real when we saw and heard your heartbeat. Thump, thump, wait, thump, thump. Real in the blood coursing through your body. We heard it, on Monday. Today is Wednesday. An unusual sloshing, slurping wave of claret, flowing, moving to where it is needed. We heard it. I've never heard blood move before.

Other people make it real. The secret that we had, is now, in the public. The doctor, our families, upon release of the very real news, somehow confirmed it to us. Before we were pregnant, now we're having a baby. A big difference to me, little one. Your name made it real too. Your gender made it real. It's really happening.

Your Ma said this morning that I was drinking pomegranate juice again because I want, or wanted another one of you, another story, another little one. I don't know. Do I? Maybe. We've got you though, and you're real. Realer, far realer on the ninety-fourth page than on the first. To think of another now would be remiss. Ungrateful, even. Greedy, maybe. You're an only one, right now, that's all you need to know, like Dadda and Dadda's Dadda.

I can only imagine now, shuffling through this apartment. Only imagination, not reality. Not real. Another person living with us. It makes you sound like a lodger. Ten more fingers, ten more toes. Where will we put your bed? Next to our bed, I suppose. Where will you eat your food? I don't know. Where will you play? Everywhere, I guess. Where will you jiggle and wriggle those ten new toes?

I can hear the wind, quietly vibrating through all. I can hear machines, cars, things unseen. You will hear these same sounds, reverberating in your eardrums, sending messages to your brain. We've seen your brain too. In detail. Several times, in fact. The sounds will reach it, convey their messages, but the thoughts will remain cloudy. You shall hear the wind, but not know that it is the wind. When I speak, you will not know that it is English (or poorly pronounced German). The word 'pencil' will seem as obtuse a concept to you as the word 'paddynoddy' (which is an old English word, which means a lengthy or long-winded story that goes nowhere and might not even be true. Sounds familiar?). No doubt, we will speak to you in a baby-voice.

"A-do-do-do-do-do".
Why parents do this, I've never quite understood. But perhaps it is better than speaking completely normally to a toddler.
"Good morning, Emily. I trust that you slept well? Now, would you please do me an almighty favour, and please drink your milk? There's a good chap".
But then why would I start talking to you like that either? Either way, it will all be just a heap of noise, just garbled sounds, which, in turn will prepare you for adult life… which I'm sorry, to tell you, will at times, seem all *too* real.

I have a picture of you on my phone. I've looked at it constantly, since Monday. When I press 'photos' on my phone, as I'm doing now, there are 1086 photos springing up at me. I click on 'All Photos'. Hold on a second…
It's a little slow.
The last four involved a coconut. Three pictures with penguins and one with your Ma, holding it. She is dressed in a white open shirt, over a white 'top'. The side of the piano is on the left of the photo. Her left hand is on her lower back (her back, which now aches), the coconut, meanwhile, is in her right hand. The lamps on the ceiling are casting a chain-like pattern on the wall, behind her. She is smiling, quite naturally, at the camera. You are also, technically, in this picture. Real.

I press the phone to go back to 'All photos'. I see your face. I click on the picture next to the coconut (soon, there will be pictures of a grapefruit on this phone, next to plastic penguins, being held by your Ma, photographed by me). This is now week twenty-three. You are (very roughly) the same size as a grapefruit.

Now I see your nose
Now I see your lips

A closed left eye
Two hands
Held up, like a boxer's
Black and white
I zoom in, and out
It's you
Real you.

We also have about forty other pictures of you, in the womb, but this is my favourite, right now, not least because in the vast majority of the others, to be honest, I haven't got the foggiest just what the hell I'm looking at... But you do have, or seem to have, a very photogenic femur and spine. At least, I think so, because we have several photos of these 'things'.

The phone turns itself off. On again. Swipe the screen. There you are. Our daughter. As real as can be.

I've seen the bed you will be born in. I've seen on screens bones and hands and a face, moving in and out of the picture. I've seen the bed you will sleep in.

Lately, I've felt you more. Vague touches, brief sparks, momentary realizations, real illusions. Move for me, dance for me, touch us, turn and tumble, trade away our dream world, and make it...

It must be real, I've seen you, I've felt you...

Seventeen

It's me again. I'm back. After three weeks. Twenty-one days of not writing to you, little one. Maybe I wanted, or needed, a little break from it. I don't know. I was ill for a week and a half, and there have been plenty of visitors. Three of my friends, two of your Ma's friends (our friends, all of them, I should say). And then we went away to Puglia for four days.

And now these slow, quiet three thoughtful days, after the frenzy of all the voices. Tonight, it's just me and your Ma, with Pepper making occasional cameo appearances, and you, our one, kicking and moving inside your Ma. Maybe I'm making excuses for the lack of letters in your honour, a certain guilt has been creeping up inside me, revealing the question; Am I not writing now because I take you for granted? Already moving my mind into other directions? This is the guilt trip I give myself a ticket for. I associate not writing to you with not paying you enough attention. But I do tell myself that I have sang to you. A little. 'All my lovin' and 'Dream a little dream of me', the latter on a beach, three days ago, half asleep, from a confused night of sleeping in a tiny tent, lying on a rug, the sea's fizzing noises lulling us back to sweet sleep. And we've bought you more clothes. You shall be a most stylish and fashionable baby. And I wait, eagerly for your kicks, as your Ma feels them so clearly, I feel less so. On the outside I am, the man, looking for his role in all this, his part to play in all this incredible operatic pregnancy (for one night only) performance. I wait for you, my hand to your feet, your Ma's belly in the middle.

The people have gone, and the sea is now unseen. In two weeks, you will travel again to Colombia, and then to New York with your Ma. I will stay in Rome, our home that very often does not feel like a home, more like an extended vacation, apart from our work.

You are the size of a kale this week. A cauliflower last week. Bigger than a fist now. Approaching the same size as a human adult head. Yet, all of you is this size, I remind myself. I picked up the cauliflower I bought in your honour. I picked up the little 'suit' we bought for you. I look at kids, subtly, babies, infant girls, who pass by, in the dusty streets. I imagine. I try to let my imagination lead me to you. If anything, I think of you too much. Has any man been more keen to see his daughter, I wonder? I look at the kitchen floor, and imagine your small steps on it, and then remind my dim-self that this event will be years in coming, and will not be here anyway. Strange days. Waiting, thoughtfully.

You should know that your Ma has written to you too, a few pages, in German, of course, in her neat handwriting, while she overlooked the deep azure-blue Puglia sea. I fear there may be more sense in her few pages, than in my one hundred (for this is indeed page one hundred, in this odyssey of mine). To be a girl and then a woman in this world, is complicated and challenging. Your Ma, like any smart human is a feminist, and me even more so these days, while I await a daughter. I am most certainly unqualified to tell you, but, yes, I should try, you may be seen as the underdog, the less strong, even the less likely, sometimes. More equipped for feelings than forcefulness, in the past, certainly, but perhaps in the future too. Seen as a girlfriend, or a wife, or a mother, before being seen as a person, or an engineer, or an architect, or a business-person, or whatever it is that your heart desires. I've seen that heart thump and it looks damn strong to me, so I'm telling you this, now: You do what you want, regardless of anything, as long as it doesn't hurt anyone or anything. I hope you take after your Mother, and not your dopy Father, in this regard. Some may try to push you down, and see a girl, and not a person. But I feel confident that you'll know what to do with these people. Fight back, and then forgive, and then forget. If possible. I don't expect you to be a saint.

And I wish you patience, daughter. First we waited to take a pregnancy test, then we waited for a positive test, then for the first doctor's appointment, to tell us yes, yes, yes. Then the next doctor's appointment, to tell us if everything was okay. Then the next one, boy or girl. The appointments now are more regular, less waiting thankfully. The doc says each time "What is your weight?" to your Ma. Then he recommends a yoga teacher he knows. At every appointment. Perhaps, he's on commission? Then he confuses one U.N agency with another, and asks your, by now, exasperated Ma "It's FAO you work for", but not really asking. Each time, she says "No, WFP". We smile now, at his forgetfulness, and put it down to his high workload, and not, hopefully, his thoughtlessness.

Finally, now, we wait for 30th July. We wait, hands held, clinging to one another, first finger of the hand over the others. We eat, drink, sleep, hold tight, plan, kiss, love, keep moving. Keep on. Go to work, come home, the tram and the train, the buses and the walking, here and there. All the while; waiting. It's a valuable art to learn, this waiting thing, this patience. Sometimes, your Ma, or another person, thanks me for my patience, or even compliments me on it. I feel bashful, undeserving of such praise. But I find myself counting the days, not really living in the moment. Waiting, and not living. It's a shame. I rarely have patience with the noisy ones, the ones who smell bad, the rude ones, in this city. I merely breathe a little deeper, and think of happy times, past and future. I suppose it's a better solution than walloping them. I wonder if I only have patience at the school because I am working, and it is my job, and my proletarian heart tells me that I must. It is a gigantic part of the job, after all. I wonder if I only have patience with your Ma, because she has it for me (in the main), and/or because I love her. I should have more patience with my parents, god knows they have (and have always had) it for me. So, I'm waiting, yes, I am. Eagerly and breathlessly. But my simple heart tells me to be patient, so I will. And my simple soul tells my even simpler head to be a good boy, become a better man. Today I've done exercise *and* eaten fruit. Good boy, Jim. Five stars. I had the fruit in the fridge, a cantaloupe, because two weeks ago that is what you were the same size as. I bought it, in your honour. So, thank you. One hand feeds the other.

Earlier, with text messages, your Ma told me that you were "...kicking heavily and happily". I sent her one back "Tell her that her Papa loves her". Your Ma responded "She knows". These three very simple sentences (details to many, and of very minor importance to others, something less than an anecdote) fill me with joy. And it is only now, when I wrote that word 'joy', that I come to realize how often much of my writing has been about a lack of joy, or joy only appearing like a fleeting shadow. And now it is (or should be) all about joy. The very fact of the matter is this: My daughter is alive, and well, inside the belly of my wife, whom I love. I should have these words tattooed on my face, or on my heart. I should never forget them. Sarah and Emily. Emily and Sarah...

The sun is out. Music is playing outside, and inside. The drums are getting nearer and louder. Patience is a virtue. Einstein said that imagination was more important than knowledge and also that imagination was everything, that it is the preview of the coming attractions of life.

I say now, that I am thankful. And again, and again, and...

Eighteen

Outside on the balcony, my freshly cut hair shadowing the paper. Very warm. Clouds above, but unthreatening thus far. The sun on my neck, arms, and reflecting off my wooden watch. Your Ma, inside the apartment, I can see her through the open window, in the study, tidying. She's now come outside. She's wondering if I'm telling you how "hopelessly messy she is". I say nothing. Wise old man I am, occasionally. And then proceed to write down those very words, so, technically, she told you, not me. Sneaky, huh? Rather weaselly, I must say. You are here too. Inside, warm, rolling around in the belly. This morning I felt you kick, so clearly, against my ear. Your Ma now has an outie belly button, it's rather strange to see it. Like a tiny pursed mouth, shocked or disgruntled, somehow.

I've changed sides, the sun was too hot on my neck. I'll get a burn. The shadow covers half of the page, annoyingly. I groan unhappily, like my dear autistic student at the school. He was interesting to teach, as always, yesterday. I think you'd like him. Your Ma, meanwhile, right now, has the look in her grey green eyes of a person about to stop what they are doing, fed-up with their task. I think she'll stop soon but I could be wrong, she is perseverant, I'll give her that. It does seem, sometimes, that she is (or has become) a figure on the periphery of this story, from me to you. Your Ma, I write, and then seem to change the topic. When, in reality, she's the starring actress, the lead role in the whole production. A 'pregnant man' takes no real role, garners no attention, receives no additional surplus looks or stares. Not that I'm complaining (perish the thought). It's a small pocket of time, this Saturday, us four at home. I said earlier to your Ma (there she is again, with a brief non-speaking part. I must stop doing that), that we wouldn't remember, clearly, this day, these days even, of sun and pregnancy, Rome, and talking to a stomach. It seemed sad. So I write now to remember (no word of a lie), only how I see it. My right arm again in the shade, under the window, my left arm between the fine line of hot and burning. The green tin of paint your Ma put on the windowsill, almost empty now, with which we painted a wall in our bedroom, the room in which you were most likely created. Should I tell you about that room? No, probably not. What room was I created in? I don't know. I don't even know his name. Absurd. So absurd. You know my name now, whatever happens. I don't even know my birth Father's surname. How ridiculous. Well, ours is Colbourne.

There's a turquoise bowl on top of the paint tin. Where did it come from? I had to ask your Ma what the colour was called, I had forgotten the word 'turquoise', it's not like I use it much. We're talking, a little, while I write. She's still beavering away at the study, bless her. My left arm is now in the shade, safe from harm. The cat has her eyes closed, otherwise she is nonchalantly observing the cars and people going by. Your Ma is unhappy about her hole-punch. I record. She's mock-crying as the tiny paper circles, previously inside the hole-punch, scatter everywhere, a small shower of confetti falling. I laugh, I shouldn't. Her face right now is quite adorable. Sad and happy, alive and here, with me. She's scooping up the miniscule circles now, and depositing them in a paper bag, that we're using for a rubbish bag ('trash' as she says, with an Americanism I don't much care for). This is life today. Later, we will go to the protestant cemetery in

Ostiense, close to the Pyramide, to see Keats. It occurs to me, that these place names, while commonplace and everyday to us, mean absolutely nothing to you. After, we will see two Brazilian friends.
Your Ma randomly asks if I have a birth certificate.
A man in a leather jacket walks by, down below.
The tram passes, on its way to Casaletto.
A white car, slowly, winds its way down the street.

I've lost track. Your Ma then mentions a divorce certificate, to give to some authorities, which completely throws me. Do I have it, or don't I? From birth to divorce. I should do something about it. Write a note in my notebook probably, instead of writing to you. It's for you, actually. To get your first passport. So we can take you to England in September. The German embassy requires a stack of paperwork, heavier than you are. The cat is now asleep, no such worries for her. No doubt, she's massacring mice, butchering birds, flaying flies, and scratching me, in her sleep.

A colleague asked me, yesterday, if I was alright. I was quite touched, but I don't know why. I replied "yes, I'm okay", and then added, as an afterthought "Just waiting for July". The colleague laughed and nodded. I went back to work. The sun has gone in.

A woman in a cardigan walks by
Pepper is licking herself
Your Ma is reading something
It's half twelve
I ate the rest of my easter-bunny
The left corner of this page is creased
Sri Lanka is mourning its dead
The planet is spinning, but I can't feel it
I stare at these words

I try to think of another word, and fail again
Motorbike noise, car noise
New page
Flies on the wall, dancing
Italians. Noise, noise
No birds here now, gone for a limoncello
No tigers, leopards, lions, llamas
A heart drops onto my page
A woman with an awful tattoo enters the building

This is now, this is today, and you will never see it. Here, and not here. Pepper sniffs the first page, warily.

Only today, now. I tell you about today, it's enough, it's everything we have, now. The past has gone, the future will be, or maybe it won't be. The cat, the hole-punch, the pen moving, the cars and everything. It's so much. A man stares, with hands on hips, watched by me. A blue dishcloth moves haphazardly, and slightly, in the deep breeze, I now notice. It's so much. My heart pumps, your heart too. The clothes are drying, I'm slowing down, seeing the end. You need a passport, it's incredible. It's 12.40. Its Saturday. It's April. It is.

I'll finish, I'll stop. Goodbye, goodbye.
A man is texting on his phone.
Your Ma says a word or three.
The heart is thrown.

Nineteen

You are back. Back in Rome with me, and the cat, and the Romans. You went away with your Ma for ten days, to Bogota, again. I stayed. I haven't written to you for almost three weeks. You came back to Fiumicino airport, having stopped in Frankfurt for a few hours. Today, it's Monday morning. You came back Saturday evening. The last one-and-a-half days have been happy. Ten days may not seem a lot, to a lot of people. But they are not us, are not like us. They do not cling desperately to one another at the thought of separation, albeit 'only' for ten days. Your Ma cried at Fiumicino airport, when you two left. Sad and happy tears intermingled, perhaps.

She looked up
To quell the tears
But the dams burst wide
I merely smiled
And tried to wipe the waves

Those five lines, I wrote for her, to her, about us. After we said farewell at that damned airport, I had to rush back home, to get ready to go to work, to do my six hours. I couldn't really think straight. I took a wrong turn at the terminal and ended up having to unnecessarily walk quite some distance, my brain only half functioning. I got home, dressed, went out again. As soon as I got on the shaking semi-broken tram, I wrote those five lines, almost without thinking at all.

Later on, I typed them to your Ma, in my first email to her, the first of nine, over the ten days. We skyped on the other day. I wonder now if you would have any interest at all, in the future, in reading those nine letters (emails technically, but the word 'letters' feels more true to their purpose, somehow). Or even if we would want you to read them? We'll see. So I have written to her a fair bit, and now it's your turn again. I must write. My laziness is my enemy, inspiration should be my aim.

Fast forward from that Wednesday morning, ten days, to Saturday evening. This is the story of five songs.
One.
'Slide Away' by Oasis. Without these five songs, or at least five of the songs I listened to, I doubt very much if there would have been any tears at all, on my part. I waited for over an hour, standing, waiting, listening. As usual, I got there way too early. This is a defined characteristic of your Father's, getting to places far too early. I'm sure I'll do it again, in a few hours, when I'll meet her from work. But anyway, what is crying? Is it tears in the eyes? Or is it tears actually *falling* from the eyes? I was not as brave as your Ma. I couldn't face blubbing in front of hundreds of people, in that crowded arrivals lounge. So I left the tears in my eyes, stared straight ahead at the gate, at the people scurrying through, and did not dare to let my face drop, lest those drops fall, from eye to cheek.

I went to see Oasis in 2005, with a friend of mine, who I worked with. We drove to Manchester, drank a lot, then drank some more, and had a fine day. Oasis were the soundtrack of our teenaged years, their first album came out in 1994, when I was thirteen. Recently I was asking a student about his favourite music, to my surprise, he returned the question and asked what my favourite song was. I, completely automatically, answered "Slide Away, by Oasis". The lyrics are simple, but the sound, to me, is epic, romantic, impossible to ignore. The lines "We're two of a kind, we'll find a way" stand out in particular, to me. Some listen to music, some feel it. I am the latter.

Two.
'Dice' by Finley Quaye. If I have listened to 'Slide Away' for twenty-something years, then, this one, has been less than two. If you wonder why tears are something that is important to me, then let me explain a little. To be a man in Great Britain, or rather, in the becoming of being a man, in the 1990's and early 2000's (perhaps because of the 'lad culture' of the time. Beer, football, not a lot else), one was not seen to cry, much less discuss it. I do my best to battle this foolishness now. Yet the stigma does still cling onto me. At films and music: I cry. Platoon, Philadelphia, Titanic even (good god...), all brought on (just a few, mind you) tears. When I was younger, of course. Death will usually do it. But I have aged. Your Ma has only seen me cry, perhaps, only two or three times. Once, randomly, in Berlin, at some beautifully played classical music. I don't know, it just gets to me sometimes. The second, at our wedding, to 'Cucurucu', a song by Nick Mulvey, whom we saw together once, also in Berlin.

'Dice' haunted me for a long time. Let me explain, again. There was a TV show, once upon a time in the nineties, called 'The O.C'. I won't bore you with too many of the details, but suffice to say, it was about four teenagers, falling in and out of love etcetera. I think it was at the end of the first series, the main character 'finally' realizes that he loves a female friend of his. It's New Year's Eve. He runs, then runs some more, melodramatic running, past people, up some stairs, past more people, with a dim look on his face. Anyway, these are mere details. A song is playing in the background. I heard it once, while he was running. But I never forgot it, and it stayed with me, in me, somewhere. I thought the chorus went "When you close your eyes and say your love's for me". Then, many years later, almost miraculously, I heard it on an airplane. Or, at least, I think I did. We were going somewhere (Switzerland maybe?). But I may have been dreaming it. This set off a belated search when I returned. On YouTube, I watched many, many short bursts of average, or below average acting. Until finally, I found it. More than fifteen years later. There he was, again, with his 90's haircut, running up those bloody stairs.

And it's "When you roll the dice and swear your love's for me". No wonder I couldn't find it, on those useless 'lyrics finder' websites. And, joyously, the song is sung by Finley Quaye, a favourite of mine, also from the 90's. if only I'd have known. Incidentally, the Oasis gig friend saw him play in Birmingham, chatted to him afterwards, and even got a photo taken with him. A nice chap, apparently.

Three.
'Heaven' by The Walkmen. "Our children will always hear romantic tales of distant years". You can see why I like this one. I heard it, probably like a lot of people, for the first time on 'How I met your Mother' (far superior to 'The O.C', by the way), the very final episode. This may be my favourite TV show. The main guy goes to see the woman, who you thought he'd end up with, but weren't completely sure, but now he goes to her (I think he runs there. Is there a theme here?). it sounds cheesy, actually, and some of the shows fans really hate this episode, but I loved it all. Trust me, after nine years of this bloke's mopey face, I was with him every step. At first, the song is a little repetitive, and almost droning. But then the voice comes in, and the chorus is epic, legendary even. My

favourite other line, which often brings a great big sodding lump to my throat is "Stick with me, Oh, you're my best friend". It seems so honest, so real, and yes, I suppose, a *little* desperate.

Four.
'What would I do without you?' by Drew Holcomb and The Neighbours. 'How I met your mother' provided to be a real goldmine of songs for me, at least thirty from the show I listened to quite regularly. And maybe your Ma likes about two of them (maximum). But I know she likes this one. It was one of the songs at our second wedding. Did I tell you that your crazy parents married (each other) twice? Seems like I should have done really. It'll have to be two more tales for another day. We walked in together to this one, into the church. "Sometimes I wake up with the sadness, other days it feels like madness". No, it's not the most romantic, or churchy, of first lines of a song ever, is it? What would I do without you? That's a question we ask each other now, because of the song, maybe. I don't know. "You are patient, I'm always on time". She tells me that I'm both, and she's neither. Well, I'm definitely the latter (if anything, *too* on time), only occasionally the former. Your Ma cried and cried on the way into the church. A *lot*. Her poor little face, streaming, looked at times more upset than happy. Hopefully everyone knew the truth. I just swallowed the lump, as I do, too often. Cowardly. Your Ma may not be on time as often as I am, but she's braver. And probably smarter too, but don't tell her I said that, okay? Let's keep that a secret...

Five.
'Crazy English Summer' by Faithless. In England, I would work many nightshifts, from 9pm to 6am, there or thereabouts. During one such week of them, this story is from. Me and your Ma met, said goodbye, met again, said

goodbye, etcetera. For the first period of our lives, we were apart more than together. If the ten days that have just gone by, felt like an eternity at times, then I would have certainly swapped it for the longer spells in the past. Her in the Philippines, me in England. I think three months was the most. It was during one such spell. Music has always powered me through tricky times, it's no coincidence that I listen to my Mp3 player on the way to work on Saturday mornings here, mornings that I have to wrench myself away from the bed, away from your sleepy-eyed Ma. The Mp3 player would fire me up, calm me down, the quiet, or loud voices, encouraging me, or perhaps, mirroring my emotions. That week I searched for new songs. I went to a library, not far from your Grandparent's house. Slim pickings, very little of interest. Eventually, more out of randomness than anything, I plumped for a 'chillout mix'. I took it home to their house and listened to it as I lay on my bed. I listed the few I liked and wanted on my Mp3 player, and then transferred them from C.D to computer to my player. It's a short and slow song, melancholic, the constant refrain of "...and I've nothing but you on my mind" seems sad more than romantic. She's singing of a past relationship, I'm sure.

And so those long hours to and from work, that week, I listened to the songs, this song in particular. I don't know if it helped or hindered me. But it was the soundtrack for me, those cold dark rainy nights, and early mornings, when I worked demanding hours, did dismal work, all the time. With nothing but your distant Ma on my mind.
The memories flood back to me now. On a slow train to Paris, I cried too. I told your Ma that I was *close* to crying. I was listening to the song, I let her listen too. My head stayed up, the drops struggling to get down, me not letting them. Time has slipped past, since that train, and

that week. But the feelings bounce back, sadness without her, and romance in (and on the way to) Paris with her.

And the song remains.

Of course, there are many other songs with many other stories attached to them, I could list five hundred more, but I shan't. Those five framed me, rushing to the airport (just like in the TV shows, really. Do I copy TV or does TV copy life? Either way, I did really run past people, and up some stairs). We finally kissed, we embraced, I kissed you through the belly, and the last one and a half days, well, have been happy. I am happy. And have not been playing epic guitar-driven songs since the airport.

And you, little one, how are you?
Ten weeks, or so, to go
You've been up
You've been low
I've chased you around
Your Ma's belly hole
You've rocked, you've rolled
You've moved, I've followed
In ten more weeks
I'll chase no more
Little one
Little one

See you tomorrow, kid. Give us a wave if you can. On the screen with doctor N. Until then, Emily, no more tears. Not for me, not for your Ma, not for you.

Twenty

You are back, again, with me. After five days, in New York, with your Ma. You returned on Sunday. I rushed out of the apartment to get to the airport, via train, to meet you two. But the flight came in an hour early. So, I was a little late, for once. I jumped off the train, your Ma jumped at me, then we jumped back on the train, together.

It has been two weeks, again, since I last wrote to you. Life seems a little busy to me, right now, but it's a lot busier for your Ma, who is still working full-time, and will be for another three weeks. My work is dipping, into the slow summer months, students are cancelling, stumbling and stammering their way, sometimes, through the lessons. I will work for another six weeks, and then we will both be at home. Packing, preparing, pontificating the arrival. Hopefully some lie-ins too. The grand arrival, as I think of it. I've never looked forward to something so much, not even close. Maybe the closest would be Christmas or a Birthday when I was a kid, or our two weddings (one in Denmark, the second in Germany). But there really is no comparison, a new person, a whole new being, will come. I swear my mind must really be too tiny to deal with this thought, to comprehend it all, fully.

Your two English grandparents are here, staying with us in Rome, right now, for one week. They've been exploring the city, sometimes without me (as is the case right now, while I write), and sometimes with me, following my confused directions. They don't know yet that you're a 'she', a 'her', our Emily. Me and your Ma are dying to say something, to scream it out. Her, her, her. She, she, she. And Emily, Emily, Emily is her name. A girl. A daughter. We wait until we are alone in bed, and speak in low soft voices, to each other. A breath above a whisper. My Ma, your Grandma, is also writing to you. The funny thing is that she doesn't know I am too. It's our secret. She said, what she's writing, will be for your eighteenth birthday. You will certainly have enough reading material to get through. Several reams could well have been written to you, by then, I fear. Your Grandfather, Malcolm, is also contributing a little too, apparently. The idea is for him to write to you about his side of the family. This is the plan, at least. I'm intrigued by this idea, immensely. I've only ever seen his scruffy doctor's handwriting in snippets, here and there, crosswords mainly. But actual writing, not really. They are not writers, neither am I, so do bear with us. I hope you view them favourably, I feel they more than deserve it. These two people, our family. Not blood of my blood, but they've fleshed out the bones, I'd say, and that's more important.

Another Grandfather will be here soon too, next week probably. Opa Roland, with his gigantic hands (of course, I've never said that to him, that would be weird), a smile that sometimes looks childlike. Perhaps a conundrum to me in some ways? Perhaps it would be better for your Ma to tell you about him. Suffice to say, he's an intriguing character, I feel. A hard-worker, a musician, a beer-lover, a carpenter, jovial, a storyteller, old school, I suppose. Not like me, your Father, who can barely screw in a lightbulb, or identify his arse from his elbow, most of the time...

Grandad Malcolm, my own Pa, how should I describe him to you? Here goes... Intelligent, quiet (or quieter than my Ma, at least...), thoughtful, kind, slowing down a little now (as is normal for a man who will turn seventy very soon), also a beer-lover, also a hard-worker in some ways. A man of numbers, he would say. So these are your Grandfathers, sixty-nine, and almost fifty-nine, as I write now. When I was younger, I saw my Father as merely a Father, he was *just* my Dad, and therefore overlooked, entirely, the fact that he is also a man. Maybe it's inevitable, maybe I, to you, will remain Dad, and never (or rarely), James. Now, I try to see the son to his Mother, the husband to his wife, the boss he was, the brother-in-law he is. It is a mistake, I now know, to only see someone as a parent. And I wonder now, as I compare the generations (for my Grandfather was of a different generation and ilk, perhaps, to my Father), will there be such a 'gap' in character, in the landscapes of our beings, as there is, or was? Will *you* be a reader, a writer, a non-driving, non-logical thinker, as I am? Or will you be organised, efficient, with your head on this planet, and not somewhere in the clouds, like your Ma? These are the things I think about, and therefore, do not seem to repair things, or make things, or build, or do business, or gather in large amounts of income. But when all is said and done, we are who we are, and should probably strive to be the best version of ourselves as it is possible to be. After all, I may not be practical, but not many people can prattle on to a foetus, for hundreds of pages...

You are well. You are kicking and moving and growing and developing extra characteristics every week. Our first birth class was yesterday evening. Me and your round Ma were joined by 'the teacher' (how would I describe her? Hmmm... what in the old days, they would have called 'a bit of a hippy', but also kind, friendly, forty-eight, a mother of two, devoted to her work, which bodes well for us...), a Ukrainian lady, (pretty, unsure of herself, reserved, modest), and her fiancé (an Italian, Italian in a way that would leave no doubt in a person's mind as to his nationality, food-obsessed, a talker, a businessman, quite amusing, and not obviously a husband and a father in the way that some men are, or seem to be). We stretched, we chatted, we laughed a little, we learnt a little, discussed, drank tepid-tea, and stood around slightly awkwardly (although maybe only I felt that). The teacher could well be the person who takes the three of us to the 'birth house', after the waters break. Our fate seems to be in her hands, somewhat. Your Ma prays, I only hope...

My Ma said yesterday that a child is a gift from god. And I thought it was funny to think of, this lady in her sixties, as she once was, a foetus too, growing in her Mother's (my Grandmother's) belly. But why is that strange to think about? Surely one human being is multi-layered, a pensioner and a baby, multi-faceted, a billion and one sides to him or her. I am the introvert, walking in the park alone, as much as I am the extrovert, joke-cracking teacher.

So, Petra and Pauline. How to describe them? Mine and your Ma's Ma. Let's see... I can only summon one, or two, or three-word descriptions, adjectives mainly. May they forgive my flippancy (and not kick me in my bollock)...
Petra: small in stature, big in spirit, a little vulnerable, a smoker, a wine-drinker, fierce in a cute way, cute in a fierce way, funny little ears like your Ma, caring, funny.
Pauline: how does a man describe his Mother to his daughter? Funny, an extrovert in an introvert's body, an introvert occasionally masquerading as otherwise, a

Mother, a little crazy, a little fiery, also small in stature and big in spirit, big in life.

I can only describe them, these two Grandmothers, as Mothers, as wives. As only my tainted and personal viewpoint allows me to view them. You may differ in your descriptions, one day. Your Ma may differ also, today.

I'm sure that all four Grandparents will provide you with happy memories, to recall, one day, to cherish. Four individuals alike in some ways, different in others. It hasn't always been the case, that in this mixed-up world, a child is born with four (eager to meet them) Grandparents and two parents who will try their very best. In this, you should feel very grateful, very fortunate. Damn-well lucky, in fact. Shelter, food, drink, warmth, love, will be yours. The rest will be your story. To be made up with fate, your heart, your soul, your mind. Your Ma prays, I hope. And we all wait.

Twenty-one

Dear little one, these are strange days, boring days or quiet days, but also things-to-do days, things-to-get-done days. Waiting and waiting for the star of the show. In two weeks, your Ma will have stopped working, in two after that I will have, and then two after that, you may or may not be here, as another two weeks after that is possible, as two weeks after a due date is far from impossible. Yet, this day, I kill time. Tidy up, read, write, clean out cat crap, clean things, wipe things, wash things. In an hour, I'll take a shower, and meet your Ma, we'll go to the birthing house, see some midwives, and try to answer their questions, and they'll try to answer ours, in awkward English. I don't know what to tell you about these important people, apart from the facts, one of them breast feeds, *everywhere,* another woman always wears *very* low cut tops, and the other one, well it seems like San Francisco 1967 should have been her home. A well-meaning hippy sort, a 'let's all hold hands sort'. Connect with our bodies. But how? Discuss our feelings? No thank you dear, I'm English. Oh dear. This cold old child of the eighties is not in his element...

Your Grandfather and his partner left yesterday. Back to Frankonia, cooler and calmer than these climes, these chaotic streets, not like this warm dusty sweaty old town. A cold beer would be grand right now, but I'll have to settle for using up the hideous pineapple and apple concoction that we have in the fridge. Last night, we planned many travels, for the three or four of us. 'Three or four' because Pepper may have to stay with Oma Petra, in Naila. And then me, your Ma, and you, will gallivant up and down, east and west. Maybe to San Marino, maybe to Lichtenstein, these countries I know absolutely zero about. To Milan, to Hamburg, to Berlin, to Birmingham. These big cities you will see, as well as the little places; Naila, Bad Steben, Rehau, and a place called Schwäbisch Gmünd. I hope it's easier to find than it is to spell. These big cities and small towns, you will see, with your tiny eyes, unknowing and curious ears, unbiased eyes, and hear many strange accents. Brummie like your Dadda, Frankonian like your Opa, Milanese, San Marino accents (if there are such things). Oh yes, we shall be busy little bees, excited and a little frenzied, I have no doubt. But you'll sleep, poo, wee, cry, giggle, laugh, lie around, wiggle your legs, jiggle your hands. And smile, and smile, and smile, we hope...

Yesterday was Father's Day in the U.K. In Germany, apparently, it's not such a big deal. But next year's *will* be a big deal to me, it will be my first, you see. For every big deal, there's a card. 'Sorry for your loss. Get well soon. Congratulations. Happy birthday. Merry Christmas. Well done on graduating. Well done on passing the test. Happy anniversary. Halloween. Happy Easter. Happy special day, for special cases. Congratulations on watering the plants, even the one around the corner, which you normally forget' (okay, I made one of these up).

Dear little one, you're the same size as a celery. But the world is waiting. Your Ma is bursting out of her clothes now. Your Grandmother is bursting out of her own head in excitement (almost literally). Me, I think, I'm still pretty much the weird one of the family. But I empty the bins, I itch the bites, I try to stop and look around once in a while. But then I'm too lazy to even blow my nose, sometimes, and it seems I'm too inconsequential for even the cat to turn her head around at. It's hot, it's too bright, I'm hungry. And what kind of a man tells his unborn daughter about these things?

Yesterday, you were in a swimming pool, wedged between your parents. I swam, she swam, we met in the middle, collided while wet, slippery. I kissed like I was dying, and you moved a toe here, a heel there. Kick, kick, kick, kicked little Emily. We parted and I kick, kicked myself, to keep afloat in the vast chlorine wetness. The sun thumped our skulls, reddened our hides. Our bones crack-creaked in the comfy chairs. We read, people-watched, all the tattoos, all the noise, the machine-gun-chitter-chatter-Italian in our lug-holes. The hot stones, beneath our footsies. Put cream on, dipped in the pool again, swam and swam like sweaty lethargic dolphins. Dipped down into the pool's bottom, pushed up to the surface for a kiss, and then parted again. Back to the chairs, the towels. The drying off and then the books again. Real life on land.

How do you feel about leaving Rome? It'll be Arrivederci Roma in not long now. I hope we can come back one day soon. To show you the sea, the swimming pools, the broken trams, the hurtling buses, everything all at once, and I hope you'll see it all with adult eyes too, coupled with a child's excitement, which I do hope you'll inherit from me. I'll show you the cacio e pepe, the carbonara, the pizzas, the puddings, the gelato. Ohh, the gelato, yes. The Pantheon, the Vatican, the curving streets, the Colosseo. The pope will want to see you too, I'm sure. We'll tell him to book an appointment. The pretty boys too, I'm sure, I'll have to resort to violent means to push them all away. We'll go to Prada, Gucci, Armani, Versace (just to look, mind you, Dadda's not a millionaire, sadly for you). We'll peddle in Pamphili. Go to Villa Borghese, piazza Navona, piazza del Popolo. It's only fair. If you care to listen, I'll tell you about Caravaggio. If you couldn't give a crap, I'll try to shut my yap (I promise). Will you notice the dust in the dying light at 5pm in springtime? Will you chuck a coin or two, to the homeless men? It's a big old city, and I'm sure there will be something to see, something to your liking, something for your irises. Yes, we'll return to Rome, in the future, one fine sun-splashed day. It's only fair, you've made it an even more special city, for us.

But only two or three weeks out of the belly, and then we'll take you far from here. We must try to be fair to family and friends. The distant, but dear people, whose efforts will shape our futures further.

As surely as these pages pile, you know as well as I, that they are for me, and your Ma, as much as they are for you.

Six weeks seems like a cruel eternity, sometimes, Emily. I'm hot and hungry, and lethargic too, and apathetic to many, many things. But to you, I remain,
Your Father,
bitten, yet unbroken.

Twenty-two

I'm sitting at the piano. Writing, with pen, trying not to leave the page. I grabbed some paper and a pen. I don't even know the date. 25th? 26th? I'm ill, sweaty, distracted, confused. No plan and no idea what to write to you, to tell you, today. John Coltrane's album, 'A Love Supreme' is playing. Jazz, old jazz. Pepper is on the sofa, behind me, plotting, eyes almost closed, studying me, she's okay with crazy and confusing music, I think. Loud saxophones howl and throb through the apartment. My unrecovered broken thumb is hurting already, after barely ten lines.

Oh well. I've got a cold or a flu, or something else that is vaguely unpleasant. I need to change pen. New pen. Here we go, switched to blue. "A love supreme...", a man chants repeatedly, it's almost hypnotic. He's stopped now. I'm only wearing shorts. It's so hot. The sun, through the windows, lights the apartment. Cough-cough, cough-cough. I'm sweating again, the cat is licking herself. It's a long way from the old cold Birmingham warehouse. It feels that way, today. I'm writing faster, quicker, speedier, strangely, sweating more and more. The vile ice-tea leaves a putrid taste in my mouth. As the music gets more rapid, so do I. Hey, hey, daughter, little one, Emily. You are the same weight as a pineapple, today. I bought one earlier and put two plastic penguins on top of it, and then took a photo. Who else can honestly say they did that, today, in the world? Huh? Not many, I'm guessing. The piano is tinkling away, but the piano I lean on is quiet. How old are you, today, I wonder, while you read this?

Still a kid, a teenager, an adult? Hey, today, it's even possible that as you read this, you yourself are a parent. Which would make me a Grandparent... I still remember my Grandparents clearly, but in a relatively short time, it's possible that I could be one too. Your Grandparents are in Germany and England. Well, technically, you have six Grandparents. Let me explain... I am adopted, so there's four, just from me. Pauline, Malcolm, Alison, Emad. I'd tell you more about the latter two if I could. Then there is Ma's Ma, Petra, and Ma's Pa, Roland. And to confuse things even more, your Ma has, technically (again), five Grandparents, two from her Pa, plus three from Petra. Confused? Well, you've only got one uncle, but then again, you could have several, I don't know. You don't have any aunts, that I'm aware of. Sorry. Perhaps I should find out, huh? Maybe I will. It's complicated. But, the main thing is you've got one Ma and one Pa, so no confusing back-story for your generation. Or at least, not yet...

My arms are thin, my legs are not, the pen ran out, so now I'm back to the horrible black metallic one, but I'm too lazy to change it, I put on less pressure, so the writing has become even more unintelligible. Why am I telling you this? This isn't typed, it's written, wrote, scribbled. My finger is misshapen now.

Now I've gotten another pen, a new one, much better. I suppose I want to communicate with you. But I can't tell you about the stars and the planets and why the wind blows the way it does. Because I don't know. I'd like to tell you about the sun, how long it has been shining, how hot it is, how far from this piano it is. Or about the moon, or even about the cat, and the mosquito, in this room, now. The hairs on your head or the nails on your toes. I should probably be telling you about boys, school, how to ride a bike, how to drive a car, how to tie your shoelaces, how to change a plug, even. But I can't, I can't. Sometimes I feel like the knowledge I have could be written on a stamp, a small stamp (although I do know that in Italian, 'stamp' is 'franco-bollo', which amuses me ever so slightly). I know I want alcohol right now, I know I want to write to you, I know the alphabet and I know I can count a bit before taking off my socks to use my toes...

And I know me. And I know your Ma. I know she does a cute face in the shower when she looks up. I know she does a funny face when she combs her hair and the brush is close to her face. I know her bottom-lip goes up and down in a really unusual manner, when she brushes her teeth. I know it makes me smirk. I know she knows that I watch that lip, sometimes. I know that when she cries, it breaks my heart a little. I know she's a messy eater (she'll deny it, but yesterday, there was a piece of food on her forehead. Seriously. Her *forehead*). I know she's a hard worker, I know she looks like a little kid herself, sometimes, when she sleeps. I know she pulls on my ears, talks to my belly-button, taps my nose, and has all kinds of different laughs. I know she does this weird thing sometimes where she talks like she's listing something. You've probably noticed that one yourself, by now, am I right? I think it's an American thing.

The album has changed, it's Miles Davis now. The trumpet is nice and calm but I can't hear it very well, because Pepper is making rather strange noises. Now she's going back to sleep, so I guess she's okay. I'm going to make a coffee. Hold on... It's boiling.

Last night I went out on my own for a pizza dinner, after the birth course, I accidentally bought the wrong thing, my head was swimming. I swam in the lake on Saturday, today is Tuesday, I wish I was swimming now, with a cold drink in my hand. I'm still at the piano and old Miles is trumpeting away.

The coffee is done. The mug is chipped, the milk was from the shop down the road, the lady looks at me like she's afraid to smile at me. The differences in people sometimes shocks me. Every day, on the tram and on the bus, I watch them, moving, living. The gangly African lads, the small Indians and Bangladeshis, the Romanians, the tourists, the Italians. The old and the young. It seems to me that there is a gap of some sort, the young are students, the middle aged all work, and the old are retired, and never do the three types intertwine, it seems to me, or so it seems. More often than not, I've got my head in a book, and I try not to think about the heat, or the sweaty sod next to me. It is my fate, apparently, to always have a sweaty bugger sit next to me. That is my fate. I hope you are nicer than I am, I hope you have more patience than I. Why do I have endless patience with students, but feel close to combustion at the folks on public transport? A character defect, no doubt, one I hope you do not inherit. A WhatsApp message dings like a cheap microwave. The windows creak and the trumpet trumpets along. The coffee goes down with difficulty. I sniff, cough, sweat, blow my big nose. I hope you don't get that off me either. For a split-second there, I took my arms off the piano and looked up at the above nine lines. I can barely read it. Which brings me to this logical thought: I doubt if you can, either. I doubt this will get typed, somehow, by anyone with half-a-mind-to. So if you can't read it, is this all just rambling, to no one at all? Or will I read it to you? Would a teenager or a young woman even want her Father to read to her? Anything? Let alone this? A sobering thought...

As a child, I watched a TV cartoon series called 'He-Man'. I had the toys, I watched the show, I even put a plastic sword down the back of my T-shirt, then held it up, and shouted his catchphrase (of course he did this in his fantastical fantasy adventures, while I did it mainly in supermarkets). At the end of every episode, there was usually a minute-long segment, during which two of the good guys would chat about what they had learnt from the day's adventures. It always felt extremely out of place with the rest of the show, completely out of sync with the swords and the battles and all the action. Sometimes, they would even 'look out to the audience' and give 'the kids' the 'message'. Now, it seems like I remember the awkwardness more than the lessons. In fact, even from last night at the 'birth class', I remember now, more the awkwardness, and little or nothing about the lesson to be learnt. I can clearly recall the lulls in the conversation (which I occasionally tried my best to fill), the impatient looks from them as they waited for answers, to questions which were vague and random, at best. And I vividly remember their judgemental faces, responding to words of mine that they didn't or couldn't understand. So, I suppose this is the lesson at the end of *this* show. And this is one thing I hope you do inherit from me, to a degree. I don't always want to be understood. I don't always want to have to explain myself. I don't want to always please people. I don't always expect to understand people, or to be understood myself. I don't always need nods or smiles like some do, or validation for my ideas. Maybe this is my only-child-thing, or the-adopted-child-thing, or something else I don't recognize in myself. I don't know.

Just as you are made from your Ma and me, and will have some similarities with us, you will also have differences to us. Maybe you will be kind and hard-working like your Ma, or maybe you'll be cursing me for passing on my belligerence. Either way, and here is *the* lesson: Be yourself, and not like anyone else. You are the only You.

That's enough. I'm sweaty, sniffy, hot, bothered, and my breath seems to bear a close resemblance to a Bulgarian weight-lifter's armpit (or worse).

Hey, take it easy, kid. And don't let the bastards get you down.

Twenty-three

Back at the piano...

Your Ma is researching wet-wipes and nappies, for you. I am sipping moderately cold non-alcohol beer, and writing, slowly and tentatively, this time. It is Sunday. Some gentle acousticy-folk music is playing lightly in the background, the repetitive whirr and hum of the fan is another background noise. So hot. There seems to have been an almost permanent little puddle of sweat, pooled in the small of my back, for these past three weeks. Change to a lighter pen and have a swig of the 'beer'.

Seven seven nineteen. Another twenty-three days, more or less, before you come. Are we ready for you? Are you ready for us? Your Ma has finished work now, for at least five or six months. I have only four or five days left to go. There is a common misconception, among many people, that work is bad, and vacation (damn that Americanism) is good. Yet I clearly recall scribbling rather maudlin and depressing poems on holiday too, feeling just as lost or lonely in the sun, as I did in a cold warehouse or a dark rainy street (for example). And while I do sometimes tend to think of my work in England, all eighteen or nineteen years of it, as an overall waste of time, it would be foolish and remiss of me to forget the laughs, the fun, the football, the occasional visits of my colleague's kids, which would always cheer me up. With my work now, slowly winding towards its inevitable long break, I find myself fully embracing the happy fact that I am a teacher, who works in a school (of sorts), who spends his hours trying to help people. Endeavouring on. Thought this way, it almost seems like rather a noble pursuit. I am currently working only four or five hours per day, and four or five hours per week. Last year, it was five or six hours per day, and five or six days per week. So perhaps the lessening of the quantity of work is also fuelling this kind of premature early nostalgia.

Does it matter if the beer is non-alcoholic? Stupid question... I recall now, on the topic, the short stories and stream-of-consciousness-prose I wrote, at usually, three o'clock in the morning. The memory seems unusually vivid. It was, usually, a Friday night. The nightshift week finished, I would return home, to my house. My ex-wife would be awake, still, watching television, we said goodnight, then I would watch a DVD, and drink (always) red wine. And then, after the film had finished, but not before the alcohol had all gone, I would write. About what? About anything. Manic streams of paper would be filled with my inky thoughts and (at times) ramblings. I wonder if the alcohol only affected negatively, or not. I remember once, on a Sunday afternoon, probably a rainy one, I had the urge to write. Lacking a suitably plausible idea, I decided to write as I skipped through the television's many channels, it turned out to be quite a useful exercise, in the art of describing, anything and everything. I turned on the news channel and described the ongoing war at the time. I switched to the shopping channel, then berated consumerism (hypocritically). A switch to an old drama brought a scathing attack on both the acting and the script. A strange lazy Sunday, but I remember it ultra-clearly. As well as, in fact, visits to waterfalls, mountains, vast forests, sumptuous beaches. Memories are bewildering, enigmatic things. Shaped by us to suit only us, our whims and needs.

The fan whirrs, the cat licks, the pen moves, your Ma's fingers tap-tap the keys of her lap-top. A sound outside, strange, I can't decipher what it is. The noises of pots and pans, also, from outside, cutlery clanking. Later, your Ma will go to church, then we will go to see Kiwi, a tiny squirrel-like kitten, at an apartment of friends of ours. Dinner, the park, an ice-cream. Sweat and stickiness in and outside the apartment, filled with boxes now. We are packing slowly, but surely. Last Sunday, we went to a pool party, on Wednesday we went to a beach, Thursday? I don't remember. Memory fails me, only three days ago, but I remember all the words to below-average crappy pop songs, hundreds of them, in fact.

The beer is gone, the cat struts in with a half-arsed purr. Your Ma gently scolds her for some misdemeanour, this is life today. My forearm sticks to the page. The cat slowly laps her water and obstinately ignores her food.

You are the same size as a papaya this week. How are you doing? You move more and more. Your Ma gets mild contractions now and then, and has to stop what she is doing. You are almost fully-formed, almost. It is possible that you could arrive in the next three hours. It's unlikely, but not impossible. We have prepared a bag to take to the birthing house, just in case. It's week thirty-six. It could happen. In two more weeks, it will be week thirty-eight, I'll be on code-orange. Two more will be week forty, that will have to be a code-red situation. And after that? Code-I-don't-know-what.

I stopped to discuss diapers (nappies). Your Ma is checking prices on the net. I feel a little silly writing about this to you, but nappies (not diapers...) seem very important to us right now, as do wet-wipes, as does breast-feeding, and tiny clothes for you. I feel unprepared. "How many nappies do we need?" I ask (dimly). Code-brown.

It's possible that your Ma's waters will break before the end of the day and that we'll have to rush to the house. It's possible. But we don't have a mattress for your bed, and we (obviously) don't have enough nappies. Your Ma just told me that each reusable nappy is ten euros. Shit. For shit. I'm going to be washing a lot of it soon, out of these nappies, unless I can convince her to just buy the planet and ocean killing disposable ones. It's a toss-up. Either way, this will be life soon. You will eat, poo, wee, and also, hopefully, wiggle, giggle, jiggle around too. Your Ma will feed you, and this alone will take hours, every day. I will try to help with many things, of course. Life will change. I will watch far less boxing, read less, work not at all, sleep less, and think about myself far less too. The last item will, without doubt, be a very good thing to occur, a positive change. These are solid predictions, amidst the uncertainty, not guess-work. Future memories, if you will. How will we tell the tales? Tales of tiredness? Such a cliché. Tales of tenderness? Well, that would be grand. Stories centred around sleeplessness? Woe-filled monologues, told by your Ma and me, of sore nipples and dump-filled nappies? Perhaps we should skip the gorier details, and neglect to mention the colour, the texture etcetera. Some parents don't, they really don't. It surprises me...

But I hope we'll also focus on your beautiful lashes, flapping above your enquiring eyes, your soft pouting mouth, your miniscule fingers, your fluffy hair in a thousand shades in the sunlight, your chubby arms... It's too easy to descend into cutesy schmaltzy street... But I do want to be the kind of Dad who says:
"You should have seen it when she.......(fill in space)"

"It was the cutest thing! She …….(fill in space)"

And the kind of guy who just *has to* do fart noises on his baby's belly. Just because.

And not the kind who complains about his sleep patterns. Or the kind who says in a markedly negative way "Oh yeah, your life *changes*". But I suppose we'll see, huh? You'll be far better qualified than I, to tell me which kind I am/was.

These days now, these hot in-between days, will go. Waiting, researching, all the wondering-out-loud. These too will pass. And though we live through them now, and they seem to be all we have as we try to live in the moment, they will most certainly slip past us. In approximately three weeks from now, you will come. And then the memories will begin to pile and accumulate. And these weeks will turn into dust, gone from our minds almost completely, and remembered, really, only in these pages. Perhaps.

Twenty-four

Your Ma says to tell you that you can come out now...

Week thirty-nine of pregnancy for her now. Next week, the 30th of July will be the due date. The date we've been waiting for since we got 'the news'. On a plastic stick. But of course, it doesn't work like that, it's unlikely that you'll arrive on that date, more likely the week before, one fine sunny day, or the week after. We are ready either way. Or, we think we are...

Thursday was a kind of dress rehearsal. We walked to the nearby park, only two or three minutes walking, but the walking can trigger contractions (as it did today, albeit milder). On Thursday, it 'felt different', they were more painful for your Ma, more intense, more in her back, and 'closer together'. We sat on a bench, watching the kids whizz by on their scooters, bikes, skateboards, round and round they went. And at that moment, I think, we did both really feel "This is it". We measured the length of each contraction on an app on her phone. And got ready to call one of our midwives, who were on standby. We felt ready, I think. But the contractions slowed down and got less painful. So, we tottered home together, arm-in-arm, hand-in-hand. And waited to see what would happen next, if anything. Suffice to say, it took a fair amount of time for us to fall asleep. A deep and warm sleep did eventually find us, and we awoke, dazed, almost surprised that there were still only the two of us (plus

Pepper). Almost disappointed, even. We must both be patient.

It's my birthday tomorrow. It's yours any day now. That's partly up to you, I suppose, and partly up to nature. Or fate. You are now very roughly the same size and weight as a pumpkin, as of today. I'll be thirty-eight tomorrow, this *is* certain. No big plans, so feel free to gate-crash the party. It seems like everyone is waiting to see you now, and everyone asks the same questions. 'Boy or girl?' To which we respond with a slightly awkward mumble "Umm, well, it's kind of a surprise, a secret, not even our parents know...". We say it like it's an excuse, something to be sorry for. Then they ask us where 'we' will give birth, and they seem slightly surprised that it won't be a hospital. 'They' (by 'they', I mean people, all kinds of people. The shoe-shop man, a check-out woman, the woman from the garage, two women from the café down the road) are all very involved. Of course, I say 'I' answer them, but, in reality, it's invariably your Ma (the Italian speaker in this little family). We've been discussing that lately, my intentions and plans to further improve my woeful German 'skills'. My laziness and reticence is holding me back, like a burly bouncer at the front of the line. But, as she quite rightly reminds me, it's for you. Which is, at once, both a devilishly powerful bargaining plea, and also a gloriously simple one.

Next week will be the start of August, which, unless I have a very drastic moment of weakness beforehand, will mean one whole year of absolute and utter sobriety. Twelve big old months, sans alcohol, of any kind. I do this also, partly, for you, my little cherry, on the cake of doing the right thing, and becoming a healthier person. It's certainly a difficult cake to stomach sometimes, but I'm nothing if not stubborn. I think it could be why your Ma loves me, as surely she is *the most* stubborn person to have ever walked this earth. In this, I have absolutely *zero* doubts...

So, without you here now, we're still in the twilight zone of waiting, doing our very best to be patient. We build the nest for you, little one. The bed, the nappies, the clothes, they pile up in the study. It's so full up with boxes right now, we can barely walk in there. We plan our escape from Rome meticulously. Packing and stacking boxes, selling things, giving things away, so many things, getting forms, to fill in, from here, from there, everywhere. Your passport is getting closer and closer. German and Italian bureaucratic hurdles wait in line to trip us up, but we sprint further on, through wandering Kafkaesque corridors, in old government buildings that stay in decrepitude. It almost sounds a little exciting, doesn't it? Trust me, it is not.

I try to contemplate serenely the big change that is awaiting us very shortly, I try to be philosophical about the coming days, weeks, and months. But I feebly get bogged down in the details. What are we doing today? What are we doing tomorrow, for that matter? And what time do we have to be there for? I try, in these days, to make the most of these moments of selfish freedom, for myself, but more often than not, the stifling heat hits me over the back of the head and forces me to the sofa, the fan, my book. And fastens me there, a form of vast apathy. It took all the strength I had, just to get off the (too comfortable) sofa-bed, just now, to open the wardrobe in the bedroom (so far away...), to bend down (my poor old back...), pick up some paper (so heavy...), walk back to the kitchen (more walking...). And then (Oh what fresh hell was this?), I forgot my pen. I finally write now, sweaty from the hot tea I just drank (I know, I know, not the wisest choice of beverage in this heat, but my Mum told me that tea cools you down...). And again, the reason is you. Dear little one, you are slowly extracting Daddy's laziness away from him, bit by groaning bit.

And your Ma (seemingly lacking my own hindering laziness) is, right now, furthering a process, a loooong process, to find us a new home, by finding a new job, all the while, having contractions. All I can say is "Big or small contraction?". "Average" she says. I am writing to you from the kitchen area, you are in your Ma, who is propped up on the sofa. I sweat profusely and scratch dementedly the mosquito bite on my itching forehead. The mosquitos in Rome are particularly vicious. Unforgiving and downright demonic. Similar in many ways then, to the city's taxi drivers...

In the steady flow of appointments these last two weeks (since I last wrote to you), the majority have been, of course, to the midwives' house, for birth classes and check-ups. Yesterday was the final birth class. It was a kind of finishing-up class. We chatted lazily, sat on pillows, on the floor like over-grown kindergarten toddlers. We ate papaya, drank mango juice, and discussed what we had learnt. Hand-holding, this time, was thankfully restricted to the holding of one's own partner's hand. We also coloured in, with crayons. Why? I don't know. We then picked out some pre-written messages from a box. Why? Search me. Then we wrote our own messages (the 'instructor' could barely read mine), and yes as you've no doubt guessed, the reason for this too eludes me somewhat. Finally, we were asked to write our fears down on pieces of paper, fears regarding the upcoming two births. A boy, to an Italian and a Ukrainian, and you, a girl, to Sarah and James. We then cast these pieces of paper onto a fire, supposedly 'burning our fears'. I noticed that the other couple had several pieces of paper, meaning plenty of fears. I wrote merely two sentences. Your Ma also, I think, wrote on only one small scrap of paper. She wouldn't tell me what she wrote. I could make an educated guess, but I won't here. All you really need to know is what I've been attempting to tell you this whole time. I doubt very much if there has ever been a child about to enter the world, who has been so loved, so looked-forward-to. And as for fear... It's known that when Ernest Hemingway was just a tiny little boy, he was asked what he was afraid of. He responded, without skipping a beat "'Fraid of nothin'!". This is how we must endeavour to face life, little one. Head-on, looking into its lights, never ducking, never running away from it, never sleepless due to the monster under the bed, never worrying about things that may or may not happen, never overly-aware of others' opinions. Never afraid. I do not say you should look leap without looking or that you should be reckless and unthinking. I only tell you this now; Be brave, little one. And then life can be yours for the taking. And this life can be glorious, miraculous, and infinitely fascinating.

Maybe this will be the last time I will write to you, while still the walls separate us. Maybe not. In the meantime, me and your Ma will try to be brave, to not fear the unknown. She may put her hands in god's. I may silently, and even unknowingly, join her at times. Whatever happens, we shall endure.

Blood and noise and shouting and a big bloody placenta separate us, right now, today.
But clocks tick, and watches wait for the next number...

Part Two

One

I'm sat at the piano again
Writing on the wrong paper.
Everything has changed.

I'm writing on the wrong paper
Because I can't go in the closet
Because the closet is in the bedroom
And in the bedroom, now
Is you.
You, you, you
Are here.

I sat at the piano
Writing for a long time
Didn't I, little one?
Now I can't wake you.
Or can I?
I hear a teeny squeal.

A noise like an animal (means I can go in)
Tip-tap on my ten toes, I intrepidly
Intrude on you and your Ma.

Your Ma is now a real Ma.
For real, for real.

I saw you depart

After five hours, only.
Only. Only?
After the wild banshee screams
From the centre of the earth,
Via Ma's mouth.

After my tears and her tears
After the birthing pool
After I cut the cord
After I gave the cat more food because 'we might be gone awhile'
After the car ride which wasn't quite
As dramatic as I thought it would be,
Continued on the contractions
Counting minutes no longer
They got no longer.
You cannot count on an iPhone
When there is an actual new human
Announcing its majesty

After all this, there was (I swear it)
A moment or ten when I looked in
Sarah's eyes
Green and grey and beyond it all
She said with irises
And words on tongue
'She's coming'

But before then…
The pool filled
The midwives scampered around
Busying themselves
I only made sure I had tissues
And that my phone was charged

Then there was the ride home

You, in a bear hoodie
Like a sleeping, dreaming
Roman princess
(in a fake-fur outfit in August)
You slept
The mosquitos bit me, only me
Neck and face
Your Ma gave directions.
And then home.

I, with six bags, midwife with you
Your Ma, with her strength
Stepped up two floors of steps
Stepped up, slow, slow
And then finally flopped, flummoxed
Onto sweet, sweet bed.

And you, you, now, now
Today now
I must take a peek.
You're awake, barely
But feeding ferociously
Head of hair stuck to sheet
Ten toes like an old man's
Wrinkled 'n' crinkled,
All up, like an old fella

Check the nappy later
And then stretch my limbs
And then you're still here.
A little cry
(these tears tear my heart, I'm softer now.)
On my shoulder, your head flops
Arms flail around
And you have nails (unbelievable)
Which on my belly, scratch.

But I can't say a word that is wrongful right now
You can take my eyes if it makes you smile
Just a little
And then back down to your
(not-so-round-anymore)
Ma,
Who is also
Mummy, tired, calm,
Sarah, Mum, a Mother.

And if I am becoming a Father
These sweet sweaty soaring days,
Then surely,
She is a Mother, right now.
This minute.

I can't write
As there's a you in the other room
Wearing a nappy I put on
Wearing a smile
Your Ma and me made

And a smile appeared,
Bashful like the teenager you will become
In seven solar system's time

And the eyes opened wide
And two moons leaped
Onto your delicious red face
I can/could/may possibly
Eat a pig leg of yours.
Or I'll let you sleep.

To you, I said
'There's a mirror
And that's you'

You looked, not surprised.
Surveying the terrain
Of your castle
And with your eyes, said
Only in my head
'Hello me
Hello you'.

And back to bed, back to breast
New nappy now
And then a whole new world
Will you see
Tomorrow.

And I tell myself
'She's here now'
'She'll be here tomorrow'
'She'll be here, even when
I'm not here'

And I've never been so
Blissfully sleep-deprived
As I am this minute.
There's a wriggling
Red person
On our bed
Not just in my head

And I'm a Daddy.
And you're Emily
Salome'.
Hey,
Centro di Roma doesn't like your apostrophe.
They tried to take it off.
I told them, clearly
'It's her name'.

They put it back.
They'd better have.

And I can't write now
Because, yes,
There's a you
Now, here
Mummy pushed
I pranced
You persisted
And then promptly, just…
Came into the world
And improved it
A little.

Little one, you
Little one, you
Little one, you
Two days old
Little one, you.

Two

I am now a Father. And not a writer. And so…

You've reduced me to poetry, Emily.

First Rome, then Florence, then Pisa, then Milan. Where the rain touched your head for the first time. I will not forget. And now Germany, up and down, round and about, seeing your Ma's family und friends.

I write now, in Schwäbisch Gmünd. On a blanket, we wait together for your Ma, under a tree, that barely covers you from the sun. Stupid tree. Your mouth moves in your sleep. Your ears don't match each other and you have a little baby acne. You breathe like a small animal. Which, technically, is what you are. But which is hard for me to reconcile somewhat, while my heart screams 'daughter'. *Not* a mere animal. A dream should not be described as modest animal. Your shoulders have some light blondish downy 'fur'. Your hands and feet seem too fragile to even breathe on, some days. Your cheeks have the softest texture I have ever touched, I think.

I do wish I could write more now. But to be present, to feel, to help, to hold, is all so much more important than to merely record. You wake slightly, with a knowing smile, and then fall back asleep. Legs bend in the way that seems natural only to you.

Sweating Rome seems a long way away today, lying on this big blanket, with you, in Germany. And finally, you fall into a deeper sleep. The nights and mornings, for me, an old schlafmütze (sleepy head), can be, a little, just a little, tricky. Coffee can be needed.

My favourite moments in these warm and surreal (but real) days are when we wake together, and we yawn at the same time. That is when I most feel that you are mine, of me, from me. Just a pair of sleepy heads, we are. You grin a grin that is alarmingly full of guile and not infant-like at all. It almost feels like an understanding between us two. Persian to Persian, perhaps.

Your hair is light, far lighter now than when you were born. And that day, long planned for, and long imagined, has come and gone. And if the five hours of labour seemed simultaneously short and long, then perhaps, so have these seventeen days, with you. It's like you've always been with us, some days. Sometimes. And yet seventeen days is relatively nothing. The pregnancy lasted nine months and three weeks. How is this possible?

You turn now, slightly, onto your back, just a little. The church bell rings loud. You are, usually, a side-sleeper, which worries me, somewhat. Earlier, I touched behind your ears, the same way in which I would do to Pepper, probably for the first time, another first. Every day for you has so many firsts. For us too.

Last night we had dinner with your uncle. The stars were out, out like they are out in the old movies. As I walked and strolled, I bounced and semi-danced, with you in my arms. I told you a little bit about the stars, above us, glimmering. Why they shine, why they look at us from afar, and how many of them there are. The world seems infinite again to me, when seen through your new eyes. Endlessly wondrous, forever interesting, and exciting. All new.

I must go. I wrote you a little poem earlier, here it is. You can give it a title. Dear heart, dear one, cry and cry until you can no longer, Daddy and Mummy will remain with you, to kiss all of those drops away. And so, I remember well…

I carried the small child
Slightly, carefully
Into the wood
Away from the noise
Of this, her and my life
Not far
Not too far
My awkward left hand bent under her
Minor weight.
I sat with her.
She was seventeen days old.

Her coiled limbs
Creased into one of my arms
While a scratchy chin held her
And her wee little wobbling
Micro head.

Occasionally and tragically
For me,
a half-hearted sob echoed
Around the entrance of the great forest
Then, quite inexplicably
She stopped and chuckled
Maniacally, to herself
And only herself

The people inside
Meanwhile
Sang and prayed
Their prayers.
I halted, and stared
At missing eyebrows
Tiny nose, tiny everything
While the hands with bizarre
Finger-nailed talons
Curled around
And made ferocious fists

She wailed again
The ancient and newer trees
All sighed
And covered their green ears

What could I do?
Except say 'Shush
Shush, shush, shush'
And kiss her red cheek
'I'm sorry, I'm sorry'.

Three

Your first glimpse of merry old England. True home of your dear old Dad. What do you think? What are your impressions? Your Nanna, Pauline? Your Gramps, Malcolm? Great aunt Val? Great uncle Lennie? Cousin Julie? You've seen some of my friends too, their wives, their kids. More people, and more and more, presents and cards and being held by a hundred souls, when you yourself are only thirty-three days old today. Or four and a half weeks as we tell all the people, who also ask "Boy or girl?". All the Germans said "So süß", meaning 'so sweet'. The English say "Ahhh…".

Time feels slightly strange here, with no work, no patterns, no routines, for me or your Ma. We try to find a resemblance of a routine for you, and with you. It seems to be sleep-eat-cry a little-rock a little-awake a little-sleep-sleep-feed-feed-repeat. My tiredness, when I am awake at two or three in the morning, annoys me a little. That I should be sleep-walking through these precious moments with you. Seems a little wasteful, a little like I take you for granted. It's not my intention. Forgive me.

The first written words, from me to you in England. Sitting in the study upstairs, at your Grandparent's house, the house I grew up in, from the age of about eleven or twelve, I think. Overlooking the garden and the many things in there. The shed, the gazebo, the bird houses, many things. I saw you just, it's four in the afternoon, your Ma is holding you, you seem slightly asleep, but are making some noises, which resemble a cat or a puppy... She is also talking to a friend of hers who (I think) has just told her that she is pregnant. I can hear their voices, and your miniscule mouth occasionally pushing a cry out. The desk is so busy. This house is full of things, and of memories for me. If the writing is scattered and slapdash, maybe I can blame the desk. The streets here, the shops, the people, all seem more alive, compared to Germany, or maybe it's just because I can understand everything that is happening.

Your Nan is also writing to you, and same as I, won't reveal her words. In fact, only me and your Ma (and a few random students of mine) know of this 'little project' (as we call it). She has also written in a book of hers, some childhood memories, about her parents, their work and upbringings, the toys she played with. And most interestingly for me, how her and Gramps (as he seems to be known as now) met, where they went for their first date, things of that nature...

The ticking clock is irritating me, I have a billion things to tell you, but this confusing thought is creeping up on me, befuddling me: Why am I writing to you when you are in the next room? My old bedroom. My writing today feels like it is being swept away somewhere, ragged and riddled with confusion. Oh, it's not actually a clock. It turns out, that it's the hand moving of a gold cat 'ornament'. The kind they have as a kitsch in-joke in Chinese shops and restaurants.

The wind moves the trees, the cat keeps on waving.

Ten-minute break from writing...
While we change your re-wearable, eco-friendly, re-washable, re-usable, all-singing, all-dancing, rather

expensive, humming-bird nappy (not diaper). As I quipped (rather poorly) to someone 'just the other day', Mommy deals with the imports (feeding) and I deal with the exports (i.e.-shite). In the carpeted bathroom (which annoys your Ma. "Gets damp", she says), with the hot and cold taps (which annoys your Ma equally, or even more, I would say), we sat on the floor with you and removed, and washed, and changed, and consulted, discussed strategies (even), for these nappies. This is life now. My god, it has changed. You are crying. But is it a 'need a feed cry'? I'll go downstairs and take a look. Hopefully Nanna and Gramps won't ask about this here writing...

"Chicka-chicka-chicka"
Your Grandad has got you on his lap.
"No crying", he says, optimistically, to you.
"Oh, alright then", he concedes.

"What are you writing?", Nanna says to me. I grunt, non-committedly. You are crying. They are devoted entirely to you, and have been, whole-heartedly, these past six or seven days. How long have we been here? They see magic in every grimace of yours. Gold in every fart. Diamonds in your shit, tiny crystals in your crying, emeralds in everything you do. Grandparents get the good stuff, they have earnt it, I suppose. I made the cappuccinos, but now I'm writing again. Faster and faster. Your Ma is meanwhile working on an application, for a job in Phnom Penh. So, it's possible that we'll be living in Cambodia, in just three and a half months from now. My Mum is ringing some sort of bell. You are close to crying. I ask your Ma if she wants to go somewhere else, so she can concentrate. My Ma and Pa go upstairs. I feel a little guilty. My Dad asks as he passes by "What are you writing?" or "Writing again, are you?". I answer defensively "I'm always writing", which isn't even true.

But this is *my* project, and I seem to guard it like a jealous little kid guards his favourite sweets. Now, you are crying upstairs. They should try to bring you down so you can feed, or I should go and get you. No, it's clear, *I* should move myself. The screams ring in my ears. I look at your Ma who looks at her laptop. If they can't calm you down in the next minute, I'll go up and get you. And, of course, it's incredibly ridiculous that I'm relaying all of this to you instead of going to get you. Live action 24-hour news reporting... They're singing something. It won't work. Or, at least, I doubt it. The floorboards creak, a cacophony of old wood. The singing continues. Now, I feel even guiltier. Is 'guiltier' a word? Or should it be 'more guilty'? Guilty and confused. I should know this...

In two-and-a-half more minutes, I'll go and...
But you're crying...
"Should I go and feed her?", your Ma says.
"Yeah, probably", I say.

Start again. This is life now.

In two-and-a-half more weeks...

I can hear your Ma talk to my Ma. I can't concentrate at all. You are crying. The floorboards creak. A door shuts, or slams. You stop. I continue. The application is put on hold. My Ma and Pa are upstairs, probably in their bedroom. But now with no baby to hold. I'm the only one downstairs now. The salt cellar is wobbling, for some reason, on the table. We're all sensitive to one another, but still, things can be said, or said in a harsh manner. It's nobody's fault. If it is anyone's fault, then it's usually mine. It's certainly not yours.
Start again.

In two-and-a-half more weeks, we will celebrate the birthday of my Ma, her sixty-third or sixty-fourth. The day after, we'll pack up and go back to Nuremburg, to stay with Oma (also known as Mimi, Petra, Pedi) for a week (or a bit less than). Then we will fly to Split in Croatia. Your fourth or fifth county in your short life. The nineteenth or twentieth for me and your Ma, together. For me, maybe twenty-eighth or twenty-ninth, possibly. Your Ma's fortieth or forty first. That's a lots of 'ors' or 'maybes'. I'm not sure about anything, am I? This life is a whirlwind, this life of yours. After our travels in the south of Germany, we took a train to Berlin, then another to Hamburg (where we saw your Great-grandparents, a rare feat it is to be able to see four generations in one photo, in one garden, smiling and blinking in the sun, on a well-taken-care-of-lawn). Then a plane to London. We took a boat with some American friends, from the Tower of London and Tower Bridge to the Houses of Parliament (where all the silly men and a few silly women go to work and play...).

You were safely tucked into the dark-blue Baby Björn carrier which you seem so comfortable in. In fact, you seem most content in car seats or being carried around various places, and less chuffed when you are restricted. Your legs flap, finding a way to kick off blankets, rugs, leggings, socks, tights. Almost anything, in fact. Your legs often move as if controlled by a five-year-old, who has found the Playstation controller which moves them. Your arms accelerate in a staccato fashion, as if controlled by a drunken ventriloquist. Your eyes seem bluer every day. Your skin has improved. Your crying is getting louder, and perhaps more frequent these past few days. Your hair now covers the top part of your ears. Your ears remain soft, and seemingly stapled, so close to your head. Your fingernails scratch the sides of things we put you in. Just like Pepper. She is with Oma Petra, for now. The trick was surely learnt from her (Pepper, not Petra).

Another favourite moment: I was holding you, on the train from London Euston to Birmingham New Street. You were happy. Smiling sweetly, smiling serenely…

Not like now. The singing is back. My Dad has joined in…

But then… You did something. It seemed phenomenal, miraculous, even. Joyously, the jolly little thing in my arms and hands… well… she laughed. You cannot walk or talk or hold your head upright for more than a few seconds, or crawl, yet, or convey much emotion, just yet, apart from crying. Lots of crying. But it seems that you can laugh too. A unique little 'Hyah-Hyah-Hyah' kind-of laugh. The young woman next to me on the train smiled and chuckled her own chuckle (more through the nose than your laugh). I said, proudly and admiringly "I think that was her first-ever laugh".

I just went upstairs to see you, and them. You were in your Grandmother's arms, staring at her, occasionally touching her mouth, gently. She was singing to you. But that was two minutes ago, now I'm back downstairs again. Now, I don't know. I can hear you crying.

I should tell you about the Portuguese restaurant in rainy Hamburg, or the Thames, as we floated on it, or the masses and multitudes in London and Berlin. The Brandenburg gate you have seen, plus the grand cathedral of Milan, Birmingham's canals and winding streets too. You have travelled many miles in your short life, little one. And made many people very happy, from a six-month-old to a woman in her ninety-second year. Life is so full, so varied…

Pause...

Nanna brings you to your Ma, in the conservatory. The mysterious bell rings. Nanna bounces you up and down. Your Ma looks up, her porcelain skin pale and clear. You groan, just a bit. Bounce, bounce, bounce. I only write. Nanna takes you into the living room, singing, singing. Your left cheek squashes slightly against her arm. "Go to sleep, little baby", she sings. You cry. The old rocking chair is next. We've all rocked you in it, in this house, some of us have been rocked in it ourselves. There is a teddy-bear on the cushion, he'll have to move his furry ass. You look over your right shoulder at me, just for a moment. Now you look outside, the quiet street. And quieten down, just a bit. Whispers in our ear, calm and slow words, you cry again, but just a bit. You look, stare, and take into your brain what your eyes show you. Cry, just a little. I take you, like a thief in the night, from Nanna, and put you in your Ma's arms. You stop crying, start to feed. Calm, calm, calm. Merry old England.

Peace descends.

Thirty-three days old today. Daughter. Micro-head. Emily.

Four

Colours.

Gold-green shite
And translucent milk
Fall from hills
Into pools, plenty
of things stain these jeans
these days.

Tears tear holes
In tiny hearts
Ventricles expand, when
You scream and bawl
Life is certainly
Different now

Breakfast is rushed,
Lunch is over.
Dinner was holding,
Being clawed, feeling even
Guiltier than twelve killers
Funny how I
Wouldn't have it
Any other way.
Funny...

It's the morning. People need more coffee, or a holiday, or the selfish old rain to stop bothering everyone. It's relentless here. We queue silently for the shower, feed the baby, rock the baby, entertain the baby, feed the cat, play with the cat, shout at the cat for walking on the table. But you and I know full well that she does it all night long anyway. This is the cat's apartment, not ours.

'Hooooow!'
Says the cat, black and white and winning
Getting her own way
Eating weirdly and walking around like she owns the place
(Because she does)
'Hooooooo'
Says you, howling wolf-like daughter
The grown-ups bicker
Make-up, bicker again
Various gestures and various grains of sleep
Shaken off, slowly, this morning
The 'Hooooow' and the 'Hoooooo'
Between you two, the cat and the kid
Gets rid of whining humans
There is no silence, no sleep
No surrender
Little sanity, little shame
Little sense
And the little sense we once saw
Has got its bus ticket
And is waiting
For soon it will be gone
Vamooshed out of here.

Oh, but
If only the rain would stop...

Quiet descends like a bomb. Apart from the washing machine and Pepper eating again (fat little thing) and phone calls and a delivery man and... I am alone again,

writing at the same table, in Naila, Oma's home. The same table I sat at when I started this 'tome'. That was the thirtieth of December, now it's October. Time does fly with you, micro-head.
You've just gone out for a couple of hours, with your Ma and Oma, to see a friend of theirs. She's an old lady, who Oma occasionally cleans for, I think. Other details do elude me at present. I have stayed in, to write, primarily. It's been on my mind all morning, various lines intertwining, haphazardly around my little old brain.

Back in Germany then, after three-and-a-half weeks in England. The Four Oaks home, with my Ma and Pa. The park, the drink, the relatives, the pals, old and the new. Meals served with meticulous thought behind them. Non-alcoholic beer these days. Super.

Leamington is birthplace of your Dadda, with its park and pleasantries. Lichfield is two stops on the train, with its tea house and its tidy old population. Liverpool is water and music and the accent, ringing in my ears like a phlegmy bell. Poor old Walsall is closed art gallery, dirty old river, closed pubs, dirty old men milling around the bus stop bogs. Sutton Park has ponies. Mere Green is memories being gradually washed away by new places and new people in those new places. Barton is more water, a Thai restaurant and now... the memory of a mild argument between me and my Ma, which also rings aloud, between my grubby ears. Guilty me, me thinks. And then... farewell. Toodle-pip to it all. Flying off in the friendly skies, with barely a thought about leaving it all again. But how much it all means to me is still incredibly difficult to do, especially on this thin paper...

Back in Germany then. Beer, bread, big women, big men, bratwurst, bread for breakfast, lunch and before bed too.

But the trees shine clear in the unrelenting bastard rain. And the colours come from nowhere then. Orange, red, orangey-red, reddy-orange, and green too (obviously). The nature never ends in these fields, these dark forests. It's not home, but it is über picturesque.

Yesterday, we saw a friend with three kids and another friend who is ten weeks pregnant. It's strange that you/we know that, when I don't think three of the Grandparents are aware of the fact. And we saw young uncle David, in his new apartment. Oma asked me earlier if I liked it. I mumbled something about it not being very homey. She nodded, but did I criticize her son?

god help the poor schmuck who dares to criticize you with my ears available to catch the blasphemy. It doesn't matter if you're thirty, three or three months old, the branch holds its fallen apple, still, in its heart, heavy from its withdrawal.
The future (yes, you've guessed it) still remains quite clouded. We're never completely sure where we will be in six-month's time. Bonn (with the Haribo oompa-loompas) could be an option, as could Germany as a whole (incidentally, Germany has been whole again for twenty-nine years, today. Fun fact), it will more than likely be in Europe, if that narrows it down much, rather than the relative wilds of Asia, Africa, or Latin America. But who knows? I'm sure you will be the first, or maybe second, to know.

The immediate future does look pretty. Croatia on Sunday for two-and-a-half weeks. I'll try to write to you again there. To Split, to Dubrovnik, to the lakes separated by waterfalls at Plitvice. Then Germany-bound once more. Then Vienna, then Budapest, then Paris, potentially. A mini European tour of sorts, and all you have to do is piss and poo and smile and sleep. A pretty good deal, I think you'll find.

This morning

Awoken by cries and catastrophe
We picked you up, you calmed
Really, rarely
Tears don't arrive
The dry wails are enough
This morning
Two pearls of plenty
Partook a moment on your irises
I kissed them away
But they did remain
(it's hard to hold a baby with one arm
and a sleepy head)
The two miscreants
Sang songs of sodden rebelliousness
Dismissed my Father's fury
Rejected my righteous vengeance
This morning...
The two Judases slipped away
With a criminal's cunning
Falling down a face of white
They slipped the noose, broke loose
Hopped the hang-man's ready axe
This morning...
Oh you cried
And shouted and screamed
And sold several sleepless servants,
Sold them with a smile
This morning...
Hearts broke, souls were skewered
And then, this morning, a smile,
A cheeky dainty precocious slip of a smile

Peeked out from the sweaty bed sheets
'Got you, fooled you, tricked you'
It said
Or, it said to me, at least
Warmed me, saved me, calmed me, kept me
Oh yes, this morning
Was a hell of a morning
The thing is, every morning,
You kill, then resurrect me, like this
With tears, then smiles
Every morning, not only
This morning.
Oh, I'm a lucky man
Every morning.

Five

Welcome to Croatia, little one.

As of this moment, you are sleeping in our bed, your Ma is in the shower, and I am writing in the living room, sitting at a desk. We have been staying in this apartment for a week and a half, with a four-day stay at the Plitvice Lakes National Park.

Of course, all of this is of little interest, to you today. You make pleasant cooing noises in your semi-sleep-state. Your smiles and laughs, earlier, as you were waking up, were beyond lovely. And then came the cries afterwards, and my shameful jolt of impatience, as I said "Hey, shush". You don't like it when we put you down, it seems you need to be picked up, played with, held, hugged. And I sometimes seem to hold this against you, my ten-week (today) old daughter. Like I said, shameful.

I could tell you so much about this interesting country. The history, the people, the bad times in the recent past (its sometimes murky history), its religion, its writers, its art. Your eyes are open some of the time. In particular, you definitely seemed interested when we went to the art gallery, peeking out with big wide eyes at the paintings. The colours, the clarity of thought, all of the many images, dancing before your new eyes. But more often than not, as with all ten-week olds, I suppose, your focus remains on sleeping, feeding, cooing and crying. It must be an interesting life in some ways and I wish I could remember when I was that age.

Your Ma is brushing her teeth, it seems to take her longer these days (or perhaps I imagine that?). Now you sleep in complete silence, though I wonder if I jinx that by writing it down. I go in to see you, your eyes remain glued shut, your arms are up, and you pout comically. Your Ma comes into the living room, I hug her for as long as I can. There is no denying it, I'm afraid, a couple's life changes when they have a child together. Less cuddles? Yes, probably.

You've also been to Bosnia (and Herzegovina, to be exact). The difference was quite startling as we crossed the border towns. Elegant minarets popped up everywhere, one or two in each small town, or so it seemed. Still the same rolling countryside, for sure, and still the same car, trundling over the same well-kept roads. But a different feeling. One of a poorer economy? Yes, sure. A quieter and calmer population, perhaps that too. And then we parked in a small town centre. German shops, mostly closed, with winding walkways around the lakes. An old woman filled her bottle in the chattering stream. Poverty. There were many refugees, from where I'm not completely sure, but I would hasten a guess at Syria or Afghanistan. We walked, ate ice-creams, drank cappuccinos. We are quite Italian these days. And then drove on. To the next town, walked and walked, with your head bobbing merrily along, in your navy-blue carrier. Up a steep hill to a mosque and then down again. Drinking tangerine Schweppes, I stopped repeatedly, an old man I felt, but only a middle-aged man I am. And then back to our hotel. Our hotel, which was a small room in a big house.

The Plitvice lakes, well, technically you have seen them, but I'll describe them here, briefly, as you slept most of the time in the carrier, apart from looking up occasionally, with sparrow eyes.

There are waterfalls, big ones, rare for Europe, surrounded by awe-inspiringly beautiful green-torquoise-clear as clear can be lakes. The water of the Maldives, but cold, and seen by swathes of tourists. Backpacks and cameras, chat-chat-chattering hordes going by. But these are my memories. And yours? Well, they probably consist of wanting to be fed, wanting to get out and stretch your fleshy little legs, wondering just what the strange languages around you were saying. It was probably Chinese, Japanese, German, Croatian. I will show you the photos, we took about a billion. One of the most beautiful places I've ever seen, so far, in my life. But you seem happier just waking up. This small act, in itself, is worthy of volumes.

As I'm sure you know very well by now (How old are you, anyway, reading this? Do let me know, if I'm not in the vicinity, I'd appreciate it), Dadda is about as useful in the mornings as an ashtray on a motorbike. So maybe my recording of this event is muddled or missing some important detail. But I have to tell you this one thing... It is miraculous. How you wake up. It usually starts with a noise, like a word, but said in a dream, remembered wrongly. A mumble of a whisper. The eyes still stay in slumber at this point, shut tightly with the night's crust. Then, maybe, the nose will twitch, the nose that people say I gave you. Then the eyelashes, the thin wisps of barely there hair, shoot up, and then fall down, like a rocket, or a falling oak tree. In fact, you are probably waking up now, I can hear you. The lip will be curling, the hands will be thumping imaginary drums, or punching imaginary heavyweight champions. The hands also splay out their fingers, like a particularly difficult piece is being performed on the piano. Then the legs join in on the fun, constrained as they are by the nappy. They jolt irregularly, they kick and create waves in the cover. It's quite impossible sometimes to keep it on you, that dastardly cover. You definitely do enjoy kicking the living crap out of it. Finally, once all of the limbs and various body parts are in unison, moving and in motion, only then do the eyes suddenly flip open, as if a switch had been flipped, somewhere in heaven. And then turned off again, just for a moment. A yawn escapes, craftily, like a particularly fox-like fox. The smell that emanates is Greek yoghurt, from your micro-mouth, the toothless cavern. And then, a baffled look at me or your Ma. But only for a split-second. Because then comes the smile. Almost hesitant at first, and then blooming. Cheeky, almost sneaky, secure in the knowledge that these two people were here earlier, or the day before. And despite their occasional lapses of intelligence or concentration, they're okay, they're not too bad, they do mean well, those two. And then the smile stays, but only for seconds. Minutes would be greedy. We pull doo-pid faces at each other and then say almost simultaneously "Look, she's smiling". You coo, and create fools of rational people. You and that smile of yours.

Why talk or write to you of global warming, or civil wars, or man's misery, piling on top of more and more? Why worry you with statistics and scary stories? I've decided that the world should remain heavenly, at least for a year or two (or three or four). The earth's problems can perhaps wait a little while longer, for you, in my eyes at least, its finest inhabitant. Yes, I could worry that you are capable of great bad as well as great good. You are a human, so yes, sadly, you are, I'm afraid. But you are also only ten weeks old, and so all that stuff can wait. The saddest day will not be your first heartbreak, that will be trivial in time and remembered, eventually, with a smile. Or your first broken bone, or poorly stomach. Mostly recoverable, and perhaps character strengthening. Or even when you eventually realize that Dadda is Santa Claus and the Easter Bunny and the Tooth Fairy (and now I do wonder if I could change my career path dramatically, from teacher to Tooth Fairy, there would certainly be more holidays and… Food for thought…). The saddest day won't even be when you say 'goodbye for good' to me or your Ma. Children are meant to bury their parents, the other way around is diabolical to even think about. No. the saddest day will be when you realize that life (or this life, at least, depending on what you believe) is finite, that it has a stopwatch, running. That the sunsets have a number, that the days do too. But this can also be your greatest day, if then, you realize, that you must, that you have to: Take the day, take this life, do with it what you wish, take the bull by the bollocks and run, run, run…

Yesterday we rented bikes and rode them up and down hills and roads and along the sea (and nearly *in* the sea in Dadda's case. Pesky bikes…). After an hour or two of this lovely little excursion, we stopped at a beach. Shimmering stones greeted us at the water's edge, lovely to see but a right bugger under a bare foot. We stopped our bikes with a firm brake, walked totteringly to a shady spot, and then kicked the kick-stands, so the bikes stayed upright and we could recline. We put you down on our beach towel. You kicked, and probably wondered just where in the hell we had taken you now. We sensed a photo opportunity, or ten. We stripped you of your 'body' and tights. Nude as a cherub you were. And then put on your swimsuit, a present from England (from the English island people). I, meanwhile, changed hurriedly behind some old hastily arranged partition, into my swim shorts. The stones, in their millions, sang angry songs on the soles of my feet. I didn't hear them just then though, as I carried you, ultra-carefully, into the sea. Your Ma prepared her camera, I shouted "Mine too". Your bare back, I covered with one hand, and put my other one in a place to support you. I didn't even notice the chilly water around my ankles, then my shins, then up to my old knees. Your (camera toting) Ma moved me. "Left a bit, no, forward a bit, back a bit". I tried to turn you around on my chest. She snapped away. For posterity's sake, I suppose. I then lumbered back up the stones, impromptu photo session over, handed you to your Ma. "Have you got her? Yeah?". And then flopped back into the sea, the water this time surpassing my knees, up and up, to thighs, to waist, to goolies, to belly. Cold. Finally, a brave flop into the water, electing not to swear a little, as I usually do. I swam like a delighted dolphin, up and down, splish-splashing away. I remained a little amphibian-like for several long minutes, under the water, apart from my haphazardly coiffeured head. And then I stopped, and remembered. The swimming baths.

Back in the days I sometimes call 'The In-between Wives Days' (it's sexist, yes, I know, but it is descriptive also), I swam two or three times per week. Partly for exercise, and partly because I didn't really have much else to do. Often, I would breast-stroke, in the chlorine-filled pool, and look up at the seats above me (a kind of 'stands'), at the 'spectators', or parents half-looking at their phones and half-watching their kids try to swim. I would glance up (and this *is* slightly embarrassing for me to write now) and think it would be so much better (or wish, even, if I'm being completely honest) if I had someone watching me. In particular, not some weirdo, or a friend, or a parent. No, in particular, a wife or girlfriend, plus (and this is the important part in the tale) a child. My child, to be precise. Maybe I'm not explaining all this well, and maybe no one can understand my thoughts, let alone me. But anyway…

So, yesterday, you again answered my silent wordless (wet) call. Because, little one, I think you were, kind of, watching me swim.

Yes, I suppose, actually, at the time, you were crying a bit, bothered by the sun, or the lack of access to a boob or two, or something else. But here's the thing, you made a wish (okay, okay, it was a wish. Are you happy now?) come true yesterday. And you didn't even realize it. You just peed and cried and blinked at the sun.

In the pictures, I smile (and blink at the sun), and you sit happily in my arms. The great thing about us silly humans, on this big revolving round thing (or one of the great things) is that our memories tell a different story to what actually happened. The wet and melancholic man was actually wet and melancholic, but it turns out that that was just the start of the story. The dry baby (with a wet nappy) didn't even know yesterday that she was in a story, the happy ending of the story of the now-smiling man. But she most certainly was.

And so, Split…

But you like lamps better than stories. Yesterday I also named a lamp 'Leopold'. It seems you like looking at this one lamp more than the others. So, I thought I'd give 'him' a name. Lee? Larry? Ludwig? Leo? None of those names seemed to pass muster. But Leopold did, somehow.

You like looking at lamps. Whatever makes you happy, little one...

Six

Back in Bad Steben. Germany. Frankonia. I'm in a café. I asked the lady for an alcohol-free beer. She looked at me like I had asked if I could take a shit on the table. Now I have a cappuccino. This is today. I don't even know what the date is. It think it's a Wednesday. We woke late, ate breakfast. I put the ugly warm pink fake-fur jacket on you, to keep you warm outside. You cried a lot last night, and you cried a bit this morning too. We lifted you from the bed (Oma's bed) into the carrier. For some reason, your left foot always gets stuck in one of the straps. Into the car-seat. Cry, grimace, smile, drive. A red light. The red light that you always cry at wasn't there this morning. You cry when the car stops moving, you see, so this red light seems to have become your mortal enemy. These are the things we talk about, here. It's very different from Split, which I miss in a way I have rarely felt before, when returning to real life, normal life. Only, this is not normal life. I'm sitting at a table, writing. You are with your Ma, visiting her Great-Aunt. You don't have any aunts, you do have Great-Aunts though, plus this Great-Great-Aunt. We are staying with your Oma Petra, again, in Naila. A baby's life it is for you. For me, these are in-between days. But this thing is not about me. Or, it shouldn't be.

The Cure wrote and sang a song called 'In Between Days'. They are a band I like a lot, although I rarely think about them, for some reason, in the way (for example) I think about Nirvana or Oasis, the bands of my youth. The Beatles too, but they're ubiquitous, so everyone knows them. I bet even the scowling peroxide-blonde 'lady' here could name at least one or two Beatles songs. I look up to see her, but she's gone. I'm alone in this room. No, a man walks back in. And then, she does too. She's looking at me, I'm her only customer. Should I order another cappuccino? I wonder.

Your Ma cut my hair this morning. You slept on the bed. The thick bed cover held your weight. Your arms twitched and wriggled, conducting your invisible orchestra. We went into the bathroom, I sat on the bath, nervously passing your Ma my scissors. Afterwards I swept up the hair from the bath with a dustpan and brush. For some strange reason, the sight of my dark hair against the white porcelain of the bath pleased me somewhat. Somehow. Strange.

A few days ago, or maybe it was last week, your Ma accused me of being 'obsessed with hair'. She was annoyed because I kept on trying to style your hair after your bath. She flattened it all down, and moved it all, after I had combed it. She says the word 'comb' in an unusual way. It sounds like 'coom'. This also annoys her, whenever I mention it. I'm sure that every other word I pronounce in 'her language' sounds a little odd too. It was a mild disagreement. I want you to look nice, and maybe I am a little hair-obsessed. Strange. Although, I was too lazy to go to the hairdresser's today.

I ordered another cappuccino, off blonde Dracula. She walked towards me. Then I asked, I said please (bitte). But I gave her the cup without the plate, and instead of taking the cup with one hand and the plate with the other, she pushed my hand with the cup, down onto the plate. Then she said something I didn't understand. I've got my second cappuccino now. There's a biscuit with it. Perhaps there is hope for our relationship after all? Wait...

The biscuit was nice, but a little stale.

Yesterday we came back from the Czech Republic. The sixth country you have been to, so far. Little traveller, you are. The day before, we walked up and down a mountain range, the 'Bohemian Switzerland', they call the region. The Bastei is its real name, I think. I carried you up and down, but I would not sit down and rest at the top, at a picnic bench, because I was afraid you would scream and cry. You like the carrier, but hate it when I sit down and rest.

Someone else has come into the café, he's asking for an ice-cream. Miss Drac is smiling at him, and she even laughed.

Yesterday morning I bought the three of us breakfast in a Czech shopping centre (448 crowns). We (me, your Ma, and your Oma) didn't eat what we had ordered, something of a mix-up, apparently, with the order. Then Oma drove us back to Naila, three or so hours. You always get what you want for breakfast. Miiiiiilk.

Later on, I felt restless in the apartment, and so decided to go for a walk, for an hour. I took you. You slept the whole time. I had an alcohol-free beer from the funny-smelling Bio shop, and then another from the supermarket. People looked at me, as I strolled around the small town. A man drinking beer and carrying a baby. At night. In the dark. Most peculiar, I suppose, for them.

There is a fly in my cappuccino. I blew it, to get it out, but my biscuit wrapper went on the floor instead. And now the fly is back again…

Earlier we went for a walk in Bad Steben's pretty park. Autumnal leaves carpeting the wet grass. Blue sky overhead, happy. Sun with her hat on. We walked. Your Ma said I was passive-aggressive yesterday. We had a disagreement. You were asleep. I lifted your hood and checked on you. Maybe I was. I honestly don't know. The fly is in the foam…

A few days ago, we were at a dinner party, eating fish curry, being jovial. You slept on the sofa, and occasionally chuckled your 'Hurr-hurr' chuckle. Maybe it is because I am an English teacher (on paternity leave) or just because I'm British, but I'm often asked what something 'is called'. After dinner, we had cappuccinos (no flies) and someone asked "What is this called?" It was foam. Later, another person asked "Where is the place that monks live? A cloist… A cloister… A cloistery?". I drew a blank, and so, just agreed. Then he said "Ahh. A monastery!". "Ahh, yes" I said, "That's right". I felt foolish because I couldn't think of an English word before he could. And he's German. And right now, I can't even remember the German word for 'spoon'…

The blonde Nosferatu is staring again. But I don't want another cappuccino. She's probably wondering what I'm writing. Maybe she's already asked me.

Last night, me and your Ma watched a film about J.R.R. Tolkien. Quite good. He went to a grammar school, close to where your Grandad Malcolm went to his, when he was a kid. This strikes me as an interesting detail, and it's really not. At one point in the film, the eccentric professor asks young J.R.R. to write him a five-thousand-word essay. "When for?" he says. "This evening" is the reply. The next shot is of him writing diligently, at his desk. "I'm not dedicated enough to be successful" I said, more to myself than anyone else. But, here I am. I am trying.

I kid myself occasionally that I don't want to be a writer, that being a teacher is enough. So, why am I writing now? To you? Doubtful.

Another man has walked in, he's wearing dark glasses, and asks for a beer. Now he's squinting at his newspaper.

I asked for another cappuccino. She was surprised. Why? It's a café...
I'll probably be pissing cappuccino-water for weeks, the rate I'm going here...

And that's the reason I don't drink alcohol anymore. Too much, too quick, too focused on the drink in front of me. Better caffeine than alcohol though...

However, I do have another biscuit. And the fly has gone...

Soon we'll be in Vienna and Budapest and Paris together. Me, you, and your Ma. Maybe back to Rome soon too. On the one hand, I hope you'll think yourself fortunate one day, to have travelled like this. You'll say casually over a coffee with people "Oh yes, I went to London, Paris, Vienna and Budapest when I was little". You'll have to say it in an insouciant way. "And I was born in Rome". You'll have to drop that in sneakily, you should be aware that they could be thinking "Listen to her..." with ever widening scowls on their faces. On the other hand, you slept through most of London and Rome and will be far more interested in milk than anything Paris has to offer.

It will be the second time in Paris for me and your Ma, together. Not long after we met, we went together, and yes, it was romantic. A red hotel room. A maid tried to walk in on us. "Non! Non! Non merci!" we squealed at her, in unison. We made a bet (5 euros). I swore blind that the maid was a he and your Ma was sure that she was a she (I think). Either way, I lost (and haven't paid up yet). Paris could be where the angels are. It's almost as special as Birmingham...

The man looked at me when I ate the cappuccino foam with a spoon...

The Czech Republic made me think of Kafka, Skoda, Milan Kundera, and Tomas Rosicky. I do hope your mind will be more varied, more open, more receptive. I hope you don't go to cafés (sad cafés) and write about people (sad people), and judge them because of the clothes they are wearing, their hair (sad hair), their way of staring (to be fair, he's doing it now too...).

The Carpenters are playing on the radio. Your Opa is a carpenter. He owns (or, he used to own, when I first met him) two guns and an axe (ask him, it's true). The only other time I've seen an axe is when it was being held by the dwarf in 'The Lord of The Rings'. Which was written by old J.R.R. Who went to school in Birmingham. As did I. I once told a horrendous joke to a colleague about Karen Carpenter...

The man is eating an ice-cream now. The whole dismal Brexit thing is still ongoing. I don't have a job. I need to go to the toilet. I don't see one in here. I'm worried I'll forget to pay for my (many) cappuccinos.

I hope you never have to work in a café and look at a weirdo who is writing, and a fat man. But it is good to learn to be bored, to learn to think, to learn how to let your mind wander, and meander around on its own. Even if you only think about dead novelists and retired footballers, every time you go to a different country.

Your Ma told me recently, that when we are in the car, I pay more attention to the music playing, than to the scenery in front of me. Or words to that effect. It's true. A song on my Mp3 player made me think of a funeral it was sung at. Another song made me think of the band's name, which made me think of a famous photo, which made me think of... All the while, beautiful scenery was shooting past my eyes. I hope so much for you. But I must be realistic, in that you are (or half of you is, at least) the tree grown from the roots of me.

The man has gone. You are somewhere else. Not here. I should go.

Yesterday, I sang the whole song of 'The Big Rock Candy Mountain' to you. I had to look up some of the words on my phone because I couldn't remember all of the verses. I like singing to you. I should do it more often.

It's empty again. You are with your Ma. Somewhere else. Not here. I gotta go.

Seven

We are in Budapest. At the central train station. Sitting on a train, or in your case, lying down, on the seat opposite me. Your Ma is next to you, eating a croissant. The crumbs go absolutely everywhere. It's 9.30 in the morning, my eyes feel heavy. I think if I closed my eyes for three or more minutes, I would sleep for at least three hours. But I need to write. You are coughing a little, cooing occasionally, happy. From our apartment to this train, we took the metro. I carried you in the baby carrier, my bag was on my shoulder, plus I had the big new heavy purple suitcase rocking unsteadily in my left hand. It was only three stops on the second metro. The people seemed evil, somehow. Watching, staring, wishing ill-will upon us with their every intention. You charm the world with your sweetness, Emily, but they must have been the ultimate 'tough crowd'. Probably just miserable buggers. Although it is a Saturday, so I don't know.

To me, now, it seems hugely unlucky, that even though this train back to Vienna is only half-full, there is a person speaking on her phone, loudly, at the rate of (perhaps) the speed of a top of the range Mclaren F1 car. She is talking to someone, technically having a conversation, but it has been a constant monologue. Her performance consisting of annoyed, but soft, Welsh tones, with a rare voraciousness to her lucidity. Now there's another person opposite us, speaking Hungarian, I think. The volume is increasing, I might have to move.

And away we go, the train is rocking. I touch your nose to reassure me that life is actually wonderful and not annoying. I need these reminders sometimes.

From Budapest to Vienna to Regensburg (in Bavaria), then to Hof, then to Naila. Trains, trains, trains. This train picks up speed. On the train to Budapest, just a few days ago, you were extremely restless, crying even more than usual. Not calm like you are now, thumb in mouth. Your Ma prepares the feeding process. Top rolled up, breast-pad out, bra unhooked, towel under nipple. She lifts you, you are reluctant, ten sips and then leaning back, away. Distracted. We go through this process nine or ten times every day. I wrote 'we go through it', but it is your Ma who goes through it, in actuality. I merely observe. Now you wail and whine, while your Ma patiently waits. You are lucky in that it is your Ma who feeds you, and not me. In the past twelve weeks (of your short life thus far), I have realized that it is indeed her with the patience, and not me, as previously, and erroneously thought.

I did try to feed you in Vienna, for twenty minutes or so. With a bottle, which we had experimented with in the days beforehand. Your Ma had an interview, for three-and-a-half-hours. Which left me on intensive Daddy duty, walking the finely laid streets of Vienna, with you, asleep, mercifully, in the carrier. I didn't even stop at traffic lights, I shambled back and forth, Austrians curious as to why, no doubt. And then, finally, we stopped. At a (not as grand as it wanted to be) café, for strudel and a cappuccino for me, and pre-prepared breast milk for you. I swear those first three or four minutes, of you actually feeding from me (kind of) were simply marvellous. A simple, yet strangely deep, little experience. Then you stopped, and cried. But no one can take away those initial moments. Not the mopey waitress, not anyone at all.

The Welsh girl has stopped rabbiting. The Hungarian though is picking up pace and velocity. Strangled vowels and strained consonants. The train has stopped, more and more people get on. The train announcer goes through three languages worth of ignoring actual worthwhile information, and proceeds to try to flog us the 'delicious' snacks "being sold onboard, right now". This Hungarian must be rather popular, one call after another. I was actually trying, at one point, *not* to huff and puff, with these words, on this paper. But I seem to have failed.

You are calmer again, suck-sucking that thumb of yours. The hand it lives on is hovering just over your nose. Your other hand is holding its partner. Like a machine, both hands pump, like a prayer.

On the train to Budapest, in a futile attempt to quell your crying cacophonies, I attempted to invent a children's poem. Here it is. You didn't seem overly enamoured with it at the time of its conception, but I'm nothing if not persistent...

The sun and the moon are singing a tune
A shining star plays electric guitar
(you can see the whole world from this train)
The lazy grass is scratching its ass
The tree does seem to need a wee
But it is, so sadly, far from the sea
The thunder and lightning seem to be fighting
Those mumbling clouds only chat in their crowds
Then there's me and Ma, cats and dogs
Albinos and llamas, eskimo's and frogs
Spaniards singing, Russians running

Chinese chattering, Japanese jumping
Your German mama and English papa
And you, our little Roman, Emily.
Watching us all
Curious
Everyone and everything
Emily.

Vienna was stately, expensive, well planned, well thought out, a little rainy, and slightly too prepared to acknowledge its own prettiness (as is Paris, famously). We preferred Budapest. Three happy days and nights there, next to the opera house, although you only heard my style of (throttled cat) singing and Mummy's half remembered odd German songs. We ate a lot, walked a lot too, up mountains, to castles, and fortresses. The princes and princesses of Austro-Hungary may have vanished with time's lonely steps, but with just a smidgeon of imagination, it was not impossible to see jesters, wizards, brave men, and braver horses, striding and charging into battle. To a painful death, probably.

You keep on chewing that chubby little digit, eyes closed, hair messed up, left hand now pulling at your face, right hand playing the invisible violin's strings, asleep on and off, while scenes scream past the tumbling train. The Welsh girl is surprisingly quiet, and frowning now. The Hungarian chap has gone for a walk. The snacks trolley trundles up the aisle, dispensing expensive crappy snacks, and boiling bitter coffee. The bloke's pretty red waistcoat needs a bloody good iron, if you ask me. Your Ma is buying one off him now (a coffee, not a waistcoat). I gave him my remaining Hungarian florints, as a kind of tip. He didn't say thanks. Trundle on. Tumble on.

Paris soon, Germany sooner, England, I don't know when. Three months old tomorrow you are. We will skype with my parents, half of the call may well be them saying "Awwww". I feel they should see you again soon. You need Grandparents, and I think they need you too. That is the way it should be.

So Austria is Arnie, Adolf, Klimt (we saw 'The Kiss', the attendant in the gallery was head over arse in love with you. You went around the museum mostly with your Ma). Plus strudels, schnitzels, Beethoven and being confused for Germans.

I broke the sodding pen. Your Ma fixed it. I love her so.

And Hungary is Puskas, Krasznahorkai (look him up, if I spelt his name right), goulash and Atila. Lazy stereotypes keep us connected to a world we don't understand. Just a few references make us think we understand a country. Lazy and dim beyond belief, but don't tell me I'm the only one who does it.

You are still asleep. The invisible violin plays on. Irresistible.

Ostensibly, we went to Budapest for your Ma's birthday. Confession. I didn't buy her a card until it was too late. We woke in Vienna and then rushed (as we always seem to do, or so it seems to me) to the central train station to take the train to Budapest. We kissed, I wished her a Happy Birthday (Geburtstag). I said, sheepishly "I'm sorry, I haven't got you a card", while simultaneously thinking to myself 'Now why the hell didn't I get her a card?". Oh, how the guilt garrotted me. We had a little time to kill at the station. Your Ma sat in a McCafe. I took you, up and down the damned place, to find a card. I got one. You peered upwards at your silly old Dada as I wrote in it. Grovelling apologies in red ink, written in a way to suggest I hadn't written it in a café, while waiting for a frankly disgustingly disgraceful tasting 'cappuccino' to cool down just a bit, from its previous temperature of a warm sunny day on Mercury. We trotted back, my tail slightly between my legs, sparrow eyes were in front of your innocent mind, still unaware of the perplexing and horrendous concept of guilt. There were two men speaking Arabic, close to your Ma, one in a beautiful suit, and the other in an atrocious jumper. I took the card out of my back pocket, dropped it casually onto the brown faux-leather chair, and sat on it. She was reading a 'fashion' magazine, the kind you would find in McCafe's (I'd be quite surprised if Donatella Versace bothers to peruse it with much gusto). I took you out of the carrier, plopped you on another chair, took off the carrier, smiled a little dumbly at your Ma, then picked you up again. Then the tricky part. Recently, you have been attempting to, and occasionally succeeding, in grabbing things. The squeaky giraffe, an annoying monster which sounds like a crumpled-up crisps packet, two plasticky rattles, and a book (also with a slightly annoying noise). With my right hand, I carefully and cunningly grabbed under my arse to pick up the card, you lifted a little on my lap. One attempt, two attempts, a third, a fourth, all failed, in trying to get you to hold the card, to 'give' to your Ma (I had written Sarah/Mummy on the envelope). I think it was the eleventh, or maybe the twelfth attempt of trying, you grasped it with all of your might, and that was my cue to then try to sound casual as I said "Look, Emily has got something for you". You even held it pointing down. You seemed to look around casually too. In on the act.

She liked the card. Thank for your help. Thank you for co-operating. Eventually...

An hour or so to go, to Vienna. I haven't got the slightest clue as to where we are. You don't care. Your blue eyes disappear under heavy lids, long eyelashes frame them, like a masterpiece. You stretch and yawn and wait, for your next adventure.

Eight

Little one. Little one.

There are some things you should know. However, and it is a substantial however, I'm rarely brave enough to tell them to you. Like what just happened. Maybe I just don't have the words. There are, also, some things I shouldn't tell you. I should leave one or two souls intact, and hearts glued tight, least of all mine. Truth and freedom are two of the things that they say they embrace here, in this grand old city, well, even the truth has its limits. I can't tell you everything. Or more importantly, more impertinently, to me and my limited soul, I shouldn't.

But, there are no fictions in this tale. I should tell you that. This is not fiction, this is all real and breathed. I even try not to embellish or exaggerate too much. Something just happened. I can't tell you about it now.

I won't tell you about this café, either. You've heard, or read enough, by now, more than enough, about Dadda in café's, getting annoyed with people, just doing their jobs, the music playing (too loudly), the people talking (too boisterously), the people being happy (unnecessarily).

So, I shan't complain (too much), I'll only tell you tales, true tales, of our times. I just won't tell you everything. At least not yet. So what shall I tell you, little one?

Yesterday, we danced. And I sang to you. In a 'French accent'. Try to imagine it, if you can, here, now. A little background is required. A small apartment in Paris for five days. Another Airbnb, in another country, the ninth country in thirteen-and-a-half-weeks for you. Two rickety rocking sofas, pointed at the too big television, a shower sized especially for squirrels or... sorry, I'm moaning again, aren't I? I sang to you. You stopped crying. This...

As we waltz
Around the room
'And in 'and
Arm in arm
You cling to meeee
Like a monkeeeey
In old Pariiii
You cling to meeee
Your old Pappppy
In gay Pariiii
As we waltz
Micro-hiiiid, Emilllllyyyyy....

And so on, you get the picture. Well, I never said it was Chopin, did I? you must have at least three 'theme songs' by now. Quite nice, huh? I wish someone would write me a theme song. I don't feel like a superhero though....

Another tale. One I feel I can tell you. The police nearly just killed us.

We were walking, your Ma in a big yellow jacket, me in my old thin blue one, carrying small round you, in the carrier, I saw a sign, it said 'Muette di Place', I think that's what it said. Or maybe 'Place di Muette'. I read it wrong. 'Place di Muerte' (Place of death), I read to your Ma. "In Spanish, that's place of death" I said, a little smugly, to her. But I read it wrong, I chuckled tamely. Many a true word said in jest, they say… We walked on, barely one more minute. A crossing. Green man means go, right? Your Ma ahead, crossed the road. I followed. Elsewhere in the universe of my ears, I heard an ambulance's siren. I started to cross the road. Two seconds later, I fell backwards, my right leg was folded under me, bad knee creased completely, bag breaking my fall, along with right hand against the gravelly pavement. What happened? I stopped suddenly, slipped backwards, right leg jutting out, police car screeching to a halt. I remember frantically trying to pull in my leg, before the car went over it. It stopped, mercifully, just a skinny split-second, in time. I thought it was me who had made the mistake. I put my hand up "I'm sorry, I'm sorry". They looked at me, horrified. But they screwed up, not me. They carried on driving, they shouldn't have. You had been sleeping, and you barely even woke up. The weight of you dropped onto my chest, safely. My hand and knee are okay, I think, now. The police carried on, after a few perfunctory glances. 'Man and child okay? Okay. Let's go'. This is our story of the police almost killing us in Paris. And we weren't even protesting…

Another grim tale. Ready? When I read to your Ma, I always say "Ready?" to her, before I start. It's a kind of tradition now, even more so since she always mentions it. When I was a child, there was a TV programme, a person would read a book out loud… And that's about it really, I think. Before starting to read, he or she would always say "Are you ready? Sitting comfortably? Then I'll begin". I doubt they have TV programmes like that anymore, somehow. Even in 2019, as I write, let alone whatever year it is that you are reading this 'now'. So, are you ready for 'The Tale of the Blood on the Bumper'? Then I'll begin…

We were driving from Naila, Oma's home, to Marburg, near Frankfurt, I think, to visit a friend of your Ma's. Now, your Ma is certainly an all-round good egg, as am I, once in a while, but this person, well, let's just say, that when we want to say someone did something really nice, or kind, or thoughtful, we say "That is xxxx's levels of niceness". If I told her this, I think she would be bashful and deny it. Anyway, she lives in Marburg. It wasn't so late at night, but in dark old Germany, in winter, it is dark, midnight dark, at barely six in the evening. I was sleepy, maybe. Just like with the police car in Paris, it seemed to happen in slow-motion, time slowed down, just like it always seems to do in the stereotyped stories you hear sometimes. To me, it did seem, for a moment, as if a person had jumped from, or had fallen out of a car coming towards us. Then it seemed like we ran over this person, or thing. No. Not quite. "Oh god, what just happened?" I squeaked. "It was a deer" your Ma said, less high-pitched than I. What actually happened, was this. A deer ran out into the road, got hit by the oncoming car, then we hit it after, probably sealing its fate. Dead. To tell you the truth, I was relieved it was a deer and not a person. A minute or two later, I said, a little foolishly "Stupid suicidal deer, running in front of a car...". I'm a city boy. It's not every day I see a dead animal, let alone a big one from the passenger seat, as we drove into it. Your Ma said "Stupid people, building roads through their homes". She's got a point, I suppose.

Marburg is pretty, hilly, a little dark, and has swarms of students. We stayed there for a couple of nights. On the second day, we went to Frankfurt, so your Ma could do a French test there. I walked and walked with you, while she was at the language school, doing the three-hour long test, like I did in Vienna. We saw a prostitute, a cathedral, lots of things, lots of people, lots of trees, lots of shops.

Or, I did anyway. When you are in the carrier, you seem to sleep like the Sandman, stoned.

Your Ma got ninety out of one hundred on the test. Clever Ma. Une magnifique Ma, you've got.

The bloke is kicking me out in fifteen minutes.
Paris is Sacre Couer, Eiffel Tower, Champs Elysees, Arc de Triomphe, Montmartre. You've seen them all now. I don't know, you'll be going to the moon by the time you are twelve, at this rate. Mars by mid-life, Saturn by sixty, Mercury before motherhood…

A person died this week, whom you have met. This is not the thing I don't want to write about.

You saw her in an old people's home. Molly. The mother of Anne, my Ma's friend. Auntie Annie. Molly meant a lot to me, so much so that writing 'meant' instead of 'means' was hard, unnatural, strange, sad. She *is* Irish, a mother of one, likes music, sherry, a little bit of swearing once in a while. She is a lovely person, no mistake. I can't use the past tense yet. You smiled at her, when you saw her. There hasn't been a funeral, yet. I'll tell you more about her, sometime. You'll like her.

You laugh joyfully, sleep, and feed. I write, think, and sing to you. You cry too. This morning, a lot, a lot. Like you are burning, like your breath is disappearing. Tears drop, I kiss them away if you let me. You cry on. Cry and cry. You cry like the angels cry, cry loudly, cry quietly, occasionally, cry without tears, cry for hunger, cry for the world, perhaps. Cry. Then you are fed, and cry with pale milk everywhere on you, from shoulders to toes. Shuddering wails spreading the milk. My heart feels alive, yet weak, and sad, when you cry. I know that babies cry.

I didn't expect all the sadness, all the fire and freeze, in and out of me, every day. But, I have come to realize, that they must be periods of grace too, because a child who does not cry is not alive. You are alive. Very.

And so, Paris. Pariiii, as they say here. The people here, of course, vary tremendously. The McCafe girl is kind, I can tell. She has kind eyes and a smile, delicate, that does not charge you anything to see it, or demand anything of you. It is beautiful, this Paris, for sure. But it's big, and a big city, inevitably, does mean there are plenty of bastards roaming the sumptuous streets. Rushing to get somewhere, so they can be a bastard, there, too. But treading on you, as they go, that is a problem. Oh, but these bastards look like angels, sometimes, and the angels could be bastards too, sometimes. The beauty and the squalor, the noise of this city entices me. Paris loves Paris, no doubt about that, as New York just *knows* that it is the greatest city on earth. The second time here, is an eyeful (no pun intended). The first time was a dream come true, as was New York, when I saw it with my eighteen-year's-old eyes. Paris is a million adjectives, all previously described better than I can do here, by the greatest poets and scribblers that have walked this earth. I love it and hate it, which really means that I love it. And it is only my second time. It is your first. Don't make it your last time, that would be my advice.

My first was with your Ma. Ask us about it, if you like, sometime.

I can tell you many things. And maybe, some of them will be useful to you in the future, in some way, as is my hope. When you are too big to be carried around. Another thing I can't tell you about happened last week. Ask me about that too, sometime.

I think there is a strong chance that I'm going to be sick, from all this hot chocolate and pastries. Too sweet. Sickly. Silly me, sometimes.

Little one, you break my heart and build my soul. And I promised you no schmaltz, no sentiment. I'm sorry, sometimes.

I'm waiting for you, in here, at this table. With a sick belly. You are with your Ma, with a friend of hers. I know her name, and nationality, and not much else. Seems like I was born to wait for you. Sometimes.

Paris is the city with six million stories, sung in the streets, this is just yours, today. One day I'll tell you everything, but not today, not this dark night. It seems a long way from home, from here. And it is getting darker. I must leave. I must go home...

Nine

If truth is what you want, then be careful. Stupid people will give it to you. The cunning will carry on concealing it. Here is half an hour's worth of truth.

One.
Train to Germany

When the dark angel without wings
Finally came, and crashed the train
That was when the woman, the woman
Screwed up the plastic bottle
And I thought up a rather cunning plan
To kill her
(just a little bit)
Armed only with a creased train ticket...
I moved down the aisle
(instead)
And wrote this.

You, you, you were pressing your little arm
Into my throat, with force
While the wits end was at Land's End, which
Is far, too far away, on this Tuesday. Where?
Where the crumbs of people drop like helicopters
Into their daft laps
And all of this noise
Bursts panic in my Grandchildren's murky little futures.

The woman I peek at now has a large tattoo, trendy

And she is reading peacefully, which makes me want to
Propose to her, this pensioner, or at least praise something
On this pesky train to god-knows-where-steinen-höf-en-ville-en-stein-en-ville.

When the angel without wings comes
We'll put them in a zoo
And charge the kids, with their dribbling ice-creams
Whose parents, with dribbling brains
Will merely say
'The angel's got no wings'.

This is a dark thing, this paragraph
This panic
For the angels without wings
On this train today,
And the screaming and bellowing
Even the bottle screwing
Are very real, very real.

I dedicate all of this
To absolutely nobody, though
Except you, who are dribbling
Profusely, while I panic.
Angels, angels...

The thing that I couldn't tell you about is honestly nothing to worry about. I haven't killed anyone (or at least, not today... cue evil eyes...). I'm actually quite a nice person, most of the time, no, some of the time, no, occasionally, no, when it suits me. You can ask my Mum, she'll tell you. But... But... it would be a total lie to tell you that I am always a nice person.

For example. The bottle scruncher is now laughing. Harmless, certainly, and good for her too, you may think, and rightly so. But I do not think this at all, right now, not even close to it. No, I hate this woman, I hate her sensible blue jeans, I hate her stupid blonde haircut, I even hate her socks. But what I really hate is her voice, the constant noise, the seemingly endless flow of gibberish that is coming out of her face. I don't want her to laugh and talk to her friend. And for this, I am not a nice person, or at least, I'm not right now. On the other hand, this minor episode is driving me, pushing me, quite haplessly, to the pen and the page. And so, I should really thank her, instead of castigating her so meanly, on this paper. I do hope, little one, that you are nicer than I am, today, or any other day.

You are asleep, throat-punching little one.

Two:
The Jet of Geneva

The fish, most unhappy, and mottled green, and grey
Was close to the edge
As we walked along her lake
Lake Geneva
Rolexes and golden impossibilities
Looked down on me, jobless Jim
And told me that my wrist
Was worthless and warranted only
Plastic Casio
Not jewels and diamonds and dreams you can touch,
Once in a blue old moon.

More water, green and dreams
Awoke, with the swans
The jet shot up and landed harshly

Heavily
On a Japanese man's bad hair.

There must be a moral to the every-day
Work-away, traffic, red-lighted, rush-hour-ed, rabble
Of animals, eating animals.
But here there is only water falling
And that is all I know

I am childish, and can therefore only write like a child, speak like a child. Maybe you would appreciate this more if you had read it when you were four? This is your honest poem.

Three.
Reading Backwards

You creak like a door if you fall to the floor
You smell like a dog and ribbit like a frog
And stare at the cat when you tell me you've shat
Fourteen weeks old, I wipe up the gold
The green and the previously unseen

I'd read backwards if I thought you'd understand
The wink of an eye and the touch of a hand
I'd suck up the rivers and swear at the moon
If I thought it would make you not grow up too soon
I'd stare at the sun and its blinding rays
If I thought it would give me more days, more days
I'd swim every ocean and punch all the fishes
If I thought it would grant you all of your wishes
I'd kick the monkeys and look at the lions funny
If I thought it would give you just a little more money
And I'd even kill the last koala, cold
If I thought it would let me see you when I'm one-hundred years old

But here is the lesson, dear sugary daughter
The sun needs to stay and the rivers need water
(so do the oceans for the fishes to swim)
And kicking monkeys is rather dim
Pulling a face at a lion could end up real bad
And a koala's murder would leave me so sad
So I'll leave alone the animals, and all of the stars
And I can't promise Neptune, Mercury, or Mars
I can't promise the earth (shit, I can't even drive
My breath is bad, and I've had two wives)
But you can be my daughter, if you'll have me as your Pa
No cars, or stars (but you can always ask your Ma).

Your Ma, yes, god bless her weird ears. Now we are back in Naila, with your little Oma. She loves you and you love her. You laugh at her, especially when you are sitting in your high-chair, around the table. She plays with your feet, speaking German to you. You lap it up, bless you too. Now you've gone out, with her and your Ma. Wrapped up so warmly, in your 'owl-suit', an all-in-one jacket, with legs and a hood attached. I call you 'Little Trawler man' because we have to fold the hood in half, which makes you look like you are meant for a North Sea oil-rig. The apartment now, is just me, speaking out-loud, what I'm writing. Plus Pepper, who goes between being incredibly excited to have us back, to terribly nonchalant about the whole thing. Cool cat.

Your Ma had another interview this morning. We are still none the wiser. The uncertainty troubles her. This maternity leave will soon be over, leaving her in unemployment. For me, after having worked so long (too long, forever long, nineteen years long) at one place in England, I embrace uncertainty. I bloody love it.

Two days ago, we walked along Lake Geneva. We talked, discussed, chatted, rambled, all about our travels. I owe her a love poem, or fifty-three, I think. Many travels, alone or lonely or in love.

It will soon be December. Here, in Naila, that will be new. The wind will cut through my Primark clothes, and bite me, the snow could even possibly maim me. Here, now, Frankonia, Bavaria, Deutschland. I'm here now. But England next. Some annoying people there too, I suppose, yes. No water jets, but there are angels without wings. And truth. And best of all, you'll be there, too.

Ten

One o'clock at The World Food Programme. Must not forget. See you there, little one. In a few- --hour's-time.

I guess it takes coming back to a country to make it feel like it was home. Rome. Us three are back here, to the land of your birth, every corner a memory. Remember the time, remember when we were at that photo booth on the corner, trying (and failing) to take your passport photo. Remember when me and your Ma sat in that little park, waiting for little you, and I'd bother her with questions,"Has the contraction started?". "Was it painful". "Do you think this is *it*?". Remember that gelato place? Remember that pizza place? The post office where you have to wait forever, for a letter you don't want, or need. The Sicilian place where they got ultra-weird with me, because I asked for a cappuccino with my pasta. The corner shop with the cute shaven-headed little girl. The shoe-man who lent us his scales, and helped with parking the car, and who remembered your name, a few days ago. This city. This city is a special one, another great place on our journeys, these past four months. My god, we've been so lucky, so fortunate. I hope we haven't wasted it, by worrying too much, or about all of the thousands of tiny fragmented things. Back to Germany, tomorrow, which does not feel like home to me, especially while we are here, staying in an apartment only one road up from where we lived. Six days is not enough for what we want to do here, and for what we need to do. Now, it's a rush.

You've gone out with your Ma, to her work. She has a lot to do. A car to sell, people to see, to talk to, to be nice to, to have a coffee with, to bump into, and talk about you first, and then work. I am in the apartment, wearing a short-sleeved shirt, boxer shorts and socks. Trendy. I am uncomfortable, the desk has no space for my legs, and my knee is still not right, after Paris. Damn those silly Parisian police. It's been too long again, since I have written to you. I'm either too tired or too lazy, these days. Or taken up with something that is mostly inconsequential. There's a squeaky giraffe looking at me...

You left thirty minutes ago. You slept like a stone last night, we had breakfast without you. Your Ma then fed you, while I washed last night's pesto-stained dishes in the sink. As your Ma got ready to go to work, I took you, still three-quarters asleep, eyes blinking and winking, in the too-bright bedroom light. I know the feeling, I'm sorry. I put the travel-nappy-bag-thing down and spread it out, woke you up some more from your slumber, and plonked you, unceremoniously onto it. The process, repeated ad-infinitum. How many times now? Buttons on 'body' open, tights down, but not completely off (unless you kick them off), T-shirt of jumper off, one arm at a time, body off over your head, the hair flicking up, fluffy and satin-soft, I kiss your belly, now you smile a little, and wake up, chuckle a little, even. The two nappy fasteners come off with a Velcro rasping noise, I pull the nappy off, sometimes but not always having the wet-wipes ready beforehand. Only wee. A heavy load of Jimmy Riddle. I roll it up and drop it, a slight pleasing thump on the wooden floor. Efficient German nappy, clean and plasticky, on as easy as you will allow, now your legs are flailing, dancing, and decreeing that this shall never be too simple, never too easy. They move robotically too, your knee joints seem rusty and unwilling. The two clasps eventually stick to the waist of the nappy. Your Ma feeds you every time. I should do this right, it feels important.

A couple of days ago, we were in a café, near to the garage where the tyres were being changed on your Ma's car. I did this procedure, this duty, in there. A small old chap watched me. Curious, I remember thinking at the time. Twenty, or so, minutes had passed, when he shuffled over to our table and told us (in Italian, your Ma translated for me afterwards) that after his son was born, fifty years ago, his Father made fun of him (his son) for changing the nappies. This would have been the late sixties, I'm guessing. Now, he says, he smiles when he sees other men doing this task, all of the time now. He said he saw that I did it "with passion", he said, and "with love". He told us this little story, in swift sonorous Italian tones. And then shuffled back, to waiting on tables, and chatting to the other customers. If the drivers here are mostly diabolical and ever-so-slightly deranged, then they must all be very relaxed, and nice, when they step out of their racing Fiats or Smart cars. We have met so many nice people here. 'It's been a blessing', as a friend of your Ma's says, sometimes.

So, nappy on, new tights on, new body on, arms in, close the buttons. Click, click, click. Trousers on top of tights, wiggly feet put where they should be. You observe all of this with mild interest. "Just what the hell does that prat think he's doing?" Is that what you think? You even seem to be developing a little patience with me. Perhaps you might need it in the future too, you think, huh? I agree. As your Ma neared her exit, I picked you up, jacket also now on. Minimal fuss on your part, thank you. In the last few days, you have also developed another adorable habit. Wait...

My intention last December was to attempt to try to keep these writings, these pages, free of gushing, over-the-top, proud, *too* proud Daddi-ness. The 'Oh, my daughter is an angel, she's so perfect I could just eat her etcetera' kind of malarkey. Maybe I've managed this, but maybe not. I've tried to tell you the truth, which includes, and has included: screaming, crying, shitting like a hippopotamus, and all of the annoying times, the times I've begged and pleaded with you to "Please don't kick those off again for the fourteenth time, and please don't insist on keeping your arm there at that unnatural angle, so that it makes it nigh on impossible for me to put this sodding thing on, which I don't even like, and I know you hate it, but it will keep you warm, okay? Okay?". I have at least attempted to try to reveal a little of that side of things, haven't I?. But hey, here is the truth, and I promise you that. The truth is that you are bloody adorable, so sod it, I'll tell you.

You press your cheek to mine when I pick you up, at first I thought I was doing it to you, and that maybe you had no choice in the matter, but no, you are the one doing it. I think. The feeling of this small act makes me astonishingly happy and content, merely the feeling of my daughter's cheek on mine. You cooed earlier too, and tried to bite and chew on me, but we'll let that go. Your Ma is finding it a little tricky now to carry you for extended periods of time. With my male strength (ha-ha-ha) being one of, or perhaps the only thing, that gives me any advantage over females these days, I can carry you for a little longer. Maybe all of the crushing years, working in those infernal warehouses, lifting heavy things, did have a purpose after all. If so, I do wish my guardian angel could have told me about it, it would have made all of that lifting so much more bearable. But then those pesky guardian angels are like that, aren't they?

I should go back to bed really. I'm tired. But I am writing this, here, now, while your Ma is working through a to-do-list, that is literally longer than your chubby little arms, and so I shouldn't really complain, should I?

But these busy travelling days will soon be at an end. No more gelato in Italy, no more croissants in France, or crumpets in England. Germany is calling. We return tomorrow, to Bonn in the west, where we will stay for some days, and then head back to Bavaria, to Oma's. ten countries you've been to, and how many four-month-olds can say that? Well, no four-month-olds can speak, but you know what I mean. But the trekking cannot go on forever. Christmas is coming, and we're technically homeless.

Speaking of crumpets, England was a fine time with your Grandparents, only five days this time. You giggled with Gramps, chatted with Nanna, and generally entertained and charmed every last person you bumped into. Peaceful dreams were dreamt in my bed, back home, and sometimes even that is enough. Plus, the ponies were out in the park, and a red-breasted robin peeked at us, as we sipped steaming hot-chocolates, and all was well in dear old Blighty. The way I describe it now makes it sound like Narnia or The Shire. I can't help it, it remains in my blood (which means it's in yours too). The prime minister may be a plonker, his ministers mostly morons, the government may greet us with condescension and suspicion, while pleading for our votes, plus there's always the rain and the wind, and the gloomy lurking at bus-stops, and the beer-spilling alcohol monsters, fighting and spewing, and shouting, and Bacardi-Breezering, but it is home. And I do love it.

Or, it is my old home. To you, maybe, it's just another country, and you may have more affinity with Germany, or another (as yet unknown) destination. I don't know, and time (I'm guessing) will tell. You'll always have Rome on your passport, and you will always have your birthdate on there too. The photo will change once in a while, and everything else, well, that's up for grabs. The fates will do with us what they will. And that is why your Father is (currently) a non-drinking, non-meat-eating man at present. Because he needs to be around for a good while yet, or at least, as long as you need a warm bristly cheek, to rest yours on, sometimes.

It's half-nine now. The chairs outside move in the wind, the sky changes from grey to blue to grey again. The clouds meander by, calmly, even slower than the trams. There is no noise, no sound, no music, no voices trailing words behind them. This is my life, today. Yours is wrapped up in it, blending into mine, your colour made from half of my palette. But you won't recall any of this, and that could be one of the strangest things, to me, that you won't remember vast swathes of your life, whole years will remain blank, only filled in by the clumsy recollections of others. You will recall the greatest and worst days of your life when you are older, that's for sure, but will surely neglect these slow moments, the waiting, the staring out of windows, all of the unremarkable (but not less meaningful?) moments. These pages, now, will be the only thing you will have, to tell you of this day, unless a photo is taken, or something special happens to me or your Ma. Today.

You are not here now, and I am cold. And whiny. If only your little fingers were here now, I would let you wrap them around one of mine. I would touch your cheek,

check if you were warm enough, check your shoes were not falling off. If you were here now.
I will see you in only three hours' time. And my god, if for this I am not truly grateful enough to poke out all of the stars, then I do not deserve you.

Eleven

To the day. It is one year since I wrote to you, for the first time, at this very table, in this apartment, in this small city, this country, the language of it reverberating in my eardrums. To the day. You had only just lost your tail. Now here you are, a dribbling, smiling person. Wearing a mustard-coloured cardigan, with your hair parted to the right. With your pink veiny hands, with squeaks emanating from around the table, with your Ma sitting opposite me, at the crowded messy table, tapping away at her laptop with a frown on her face, her hair also parted to the right, with your stockinged legs and feet gyrating, with your Oma now talking to you, and kissing you, saying you have a cold nose, and cold feet, and cold-everything, while I think she is still wondering what I am writing, while I think up a reply for when she asks, while you drop the teddy bear my Ma made for you, while your Ma gets more and more annoyed by her efforts at the computer, while I give the bear to Oma, who gives it to you, so you can play with it. To the day, it is one year to the day, when back then you were alive inside another human being.

Ten minutes ago, we returned from our walk. I changed your nappy on the bed. You twisted and turned, to my annoyance, I said "Please!", with an unfriendly, impatient, shitty tone to my voice, to you. Thankfully, you didn't seem concerned at all. I think it was only last week, when I wrote to you, that I didn't deserve you, if I wouldn't 'poke out all of the stars', and now here I am, an idiot, who can barely change a baby's nappy without keeping an even temper. While you smile at me now, and I certainly do not deserve you, while I wonder how this story will end. I wink at you, while you chew on the teddy. I don't want you to cry. This table is too crowded, the weather is awful, the cat mostly ignores me now, I need to go to the toilet, but I can't even summon up the energy to do that. I need to sort another job as soon as possible, but I want to be a writer full-time, I want my Dad's hearing to improve, I want my Ma to be happy, I want your Oma to not smoke so much, I want your Opa to not work so much, I want your Ma to find a job of her own soon, I want my hair to always be this incredible and amazing, I want to stop masking over things with thinly-veiled 'humour'.

The benefits people of Naila want us to stay in Naila, to be able to report to them at any given moment. I say this is "a lack of freedom imposed upon us". She seems to accept it. Your Oma cuts up food, you smile, and dribble, more and more. I'm fed up of being nice, I think I'll go back to passive-aggressiveness. Right now, you are on the fine-line between creaking and crying, and now you have crossed it, and now you are screwing up my writing while I hold you, and dribbling on my hand. I tell you "Well, it is yours anyway". You throw it on the floor. I huff and puff and no one notices. Cut-cut and tap-tap, go the knife and the computer. I carry you to the mat on the floor and pull the cord for the mobile, which 'sings' a clunky creaky tune to you, more than I can do. I'm close to panic. A nurse told me once that I should write down my feelings when this occurs. That is *not* what I am doing now. You roll over on the mat, as Oma turns on the television. It's too loud, but only I notice this, it seems. No one is watching it.

I used to think I should try to be nice to everyone, and everything, but that's a lie, and I did say I wouldn't lie to you. Your Oma is now talking to you, I can no longer see you. Your Ma stares at her screen, glasses perched on her nose, frowning, silent, unknowable, right now. Tap-tap. You are now alone and crying. I must stop this writing. I must pick you up before my soul collapses into itself and falls out completely. I picture this. It's better than the TV programme.

The sky earlier had shades of custard-cream in it
The people had piercings
And couldn't manage to put their hands to their mouths
When they coughed, loudly
This image should be on the town's flag.
And the motto should be...

You are grasping at things you cannot reach
As am I
You sneeze
I say "Bless you"
I hold you
It's not so bad.

The airline lost your pram. We're going to Belgium soon. It's New Year's Eve tomorrow night. I'm not eating meat anymore.
We ate goose on Christmas day. I had to.
Tap-tap. Cut-cut.
A mentally deranged man was racist to me this week.
I don't forgive him.
He said I was a guest in this country.
Well, then, I guess I'm a guest.
He'll be dead soon. Fact.
And you are crying, crying, crying.
Sucking your thumb, dribbling on me.

Wriggling on my lap.

I'll keep on swimming in the warm engulfing noise, there is no other choice. I'll keep on feeling it all, way too much. Tap-tap. Cut-cut. I'm holding you, tightly. So, what should I tell you? What do you want to know? Thumb-sucker, still a dream, you, you, you...

I'm still reading these pages to your Ma, after each new chapter. Sometimes she likes it, sometimes less so.

You've just shat while sitting on my lap. I wait in case you 'do another one'. Or more. Our routine. You and I.

Christmas is over, but I'm not concerned at all, or bemoaning its passing. I had a nice present from your Ma, a poetry book, she wrote in it that I 'am the best Father to our little Emily'. I thanked her, I thank her now, in my mind. I sometimes wonder if it's true, though I do kiss and hold and care for you more than anyone else in this loud solar system (except your Ma, maybe).

Your Ma turned down the job in Bonn. So, no growing up in Haribo land, for you.
Maybe Geneva or Paris instead. I don't know.
Cuckoo clock land maybe. Where the birds remain fed, and wooden.

The yellow ring-pull of the tinkly mobile hovers over you like a helicopter.
The whole mat sways as you kick it. And all the animals dance away.
The koalas wobble, while the moon-faced mobile starts to look as if it might frown soon.

We went to church on the twenty-fourth, which is 'Christmas Day' here. When we got there, only one solitary seat was left. Me and your hurried and harried Ma took it in turns to sit on it. The service was entirely in German, obviously. It recounted 'The Christmas Story', there were some hymns, some to join in with, and others not to. She fed you when you cried, and I sat down then, my turn, listening closely to the pastor's unusual enunciation, his reliance on drawing out all of his s's. I understood almost zero, null, nothing. Why did I go? Well, maybe I have a different answer now than I did then.

I'm lying on the floor, while you lie on the mat, I am next to you, our elbows touch. You are smiling at me, and as soon as I write this, you stop. This is heaven, and so must be doled out with care, not with abandon.

There are two nows now
The now of now,
The now of lying on the floor with you
The same now as the now of you turning around and rolling on your now trapped right arm
This is our now
I writing, you rolling
And then there is the now that is all yours
Yours alone, now
That now sees you reading this, now
No longer rolling, now
Now you read this
Now you judge me
Now I think you know me better
Than you do now.

If there is a god, he's in your smile. If there is a god, he's in your goofy laugh, in your long thin hair, in your earth-like eyes, far away, and that which keeps me from floating away. If there is a god, I'd say…

Time to say goodbye. Your Ma is talking to Oma, I'm on the floor, with you. No more chop-chop and tap-tap. Dinner will be ready in a few minutes. There is a cuddly pig next to you. And dinner is ready now, not in a few minutes, apparently.

To the day, it is one year to the day. What have I told you? What should I tell you? Dinner is over now. You are playing the 'horsey game' with your Ma, you sit on her lap, she bounces you up and down, while making clip-clop noises, horse sounds. You giggle, mostly. Earlier we went out together, just the two of us, to the shops, for beer for me (non-alcoholic natürlich) and chocolate for your Ma (and a doughnut for me, too). I walked, carried you, no hands, up and down the empty streets, past the church where there may or may not be a stained glass window painted by Marc Chagall (I may have dreamt this though, so this 'fact' could be entirely imaginary), past the bio shop with 'wary woman' inside, past the kebab shop with the nude woman on its advertising, past the clothes shop with its stripy shirts and awfully ugly jumpers inside, past the book shop, past the half-asleep town that is actually a city, past the Italian restaurant, past the Thai massage place, past the giggling teenage girls, past the cold sensible adults, past it all, past everything…

But we were under the sunset, but, Oh, under the sunset, under the cream and custard-coloured clouds, under the pink and pineapple clouds, under them with a mobile phone, taking two pictures of the colours, in and within, under the clumsy quilt that was designed by no-one, under the fat ones, under the thin ones, the crowds of clouds, and the lonesome solitary clouds. The sunset, the sun set. This is what I should tell you about, I realize, tonight, little one. Not about the noise, not about the bothersome people, the chaos, the small and infinitely pointless and forgettable blasting of life. No. But at least you have a whole story now. Beginning, middle and end.

To the day, to this day
Last year you weren't even here
And now you are
This is what I should tell you
Sunsets and you
Butterflies and penguins
Roses and ice-cream.

Butterflies and penguins and roses and ice-creams and sunsets and you and Pepper and...

Twelve

Back in England, dear Miss partial-Persian, in the spare room of my parent's house, looking at a thousand photos all at once, sitting at a desk, overlooking the garden, family surrounding me. Pictures of me, and your Ma, everywhere. The garden down there looks sad, shut down for the winter. The first picture I saw was an impossibility, almost. You, being held by my cousin, which happened just a few days ago. My Ma is quick with photos, but as it turns out, not that quick, this time. Because the baby is not you, it's my second cousin (my cousin's daughter). He holds her, not you, at her baptism. Now I look again, and he is not smiling. She looks to the left, at something that no one can see anymore. My cousin and his eldest daughter look centre-left, only his partner looks at the camera. The youngest daughter, in the picture, is younger than you are now, her hair is parted the same way as yours, and it droops down.

Here is another picture, the Philippines. Mount Taal in the background, peaking its nosey head out, over our boat, the photographer in front of us, your Ma's bare legs, pale, with her hands clutched in front of her lap, an old watch glimmers on her right arm, the smooth red boat, with just another pair of tourists in it, sitting and smiling. A plastic advertising sheet covers our legs a little, drenched in sea water, next to the world's smallest volcano. It erupted this week, and that is all I know. I don't even know if there were any fatalities. I was playing badminton in England, or eating chocolate biscuits, perhaps.

Two books are next to me. One is the poetry book gift. I sometimes feel like I am the last surviving reader of poetry in the world. Who reads it these days? Apart from confused kids at school or guests at weddings or funerals, I mean? I read a poem (not one of mine, don't worry) at a friend's wedding. A true friend this man. This man who was a boy when I met him, when we had every day together at school. Football, badminton, maths class, beer, pubs, clubs, bad dancing, bad teachers, and a whole lot more. Thirty-five years, he has been my friend. But he still beat me twice at badminton this week, the bastard...

The other book is haunting me. Robert Fisk is a writer who really cracks the ice in you, and there aren't all that many. A war correspondent who is as eloquent as he is brave, who makes you want to be more, do more, or at least be more informed about the world we were dropped into. And about the death, the carnage, the children torn apart, by British missiles in the Middle East. Britain seems to mourn its soldiers but not its victims. I love this country, but surely the Swiss or Bahamians have less sleepless nights, less blood on their tidy hands, less burden when finally informed. It is better to know, and to not sleep, with these things, than to sleep in peace when day is done. It is so much more difficult, but more human, I would argue. Your Nanna disagrees, but then so would the majority of people, I think. My god, she loves you. So, thank Allah that you are not Iraqi, only a partial-Persian with a German passport. Thank god too, that my passport has a unicorn and a lion on it, so I can occasionally indulge myself with this ridiculous faux guilt.

A picture of you, everywhere I look. One in my eye-line, you, double-chinned, looking, bewildered, at something out of picture. Now I can hear you outside the door, gurgling, and uttering something in your mysterious baby language. My face reflects in the frame, I look knackered, a little bit of curly hair the only buoyant thing about me. Next to it is a picture of me and my Ma in New York. She smiles, I smirk. You are downstairs again now, and I'd like to hold you, but I've shut myself in here instead, with memories, with my former selves, the ghosts of me and my family. But you will always be my only blood relative. I cannot explain the importance of this to myself, let alone to anyone else. Maybe you will understand one day. Then you can inform me.

But back in England, all is well, the mud squelches and the rain lashes down, but the hoods stay up and the tea boils as it should. And now these pages of gibberish are piling again and that makes me feel splendid. I think that I try less here, I know the customs, I know the lingo, I've eaten the Yorkshire puddings and have thrown the crumpets down my gullet. It's good too, to be able to understand, I can read these faces, I can smell the parks, under and around me, I can name the birds, and can feel that the trees could know me too, if they really tried to remember. And the people, the old and the young, there is no bullshit in these Brummie voices, there is no unnecessary solemness, no wishful thinking. These people know when a thing is 'too good to be true', just as they know when 'you'd be daft not to'. This land fattens my body, and soul, and it baffles me, sometimes, that you, my blood, my bab, are only one-quarter English/British. But despite all of this, these robins, these grassy rugby fields, this Cadbury's chocolate, the curry and the cakes, despite all of this, I don't want to live here permanently. I'd prefer Brussels or Geneva or Paris or Prague, or even back to Prussia. Why? Because biscuits can get stale and cakes can go soft. Or is it the other way around?

Incidentally. F.Y.I, just so you know. We're still homeless, technically, hopping from one place to another, like frenetic frogs, through the homes of family and friends. Berlin next, maybe. Then Athens or Rwanda or Beirut. Us three wallies could end up anywhere, and yes, that fact still fascinates me, and frustrates your poor Ma. And you? Well, you don't care one jot. Not really, as long as you can bite the head of Sophie the giraffe and can chew on your cardigan's soggy woollen sleeves.

Speaking of Belgium, yes, that was your eleventh country. Brussels, Gent, Bruges, and Antwerp. Seen from your baby seat, in the hire car, or from the trusty blue carrier. Waffles and chocolate and mussels and fries. Jean-Claude Van Damme, Tin-Tin, and Doctor Evil drinking pints of Stella Artois, just around the corner from the E.U. While the continent bothers itself about Brexit, I read poetry and blow raspberries on your belly. Who's the fool? I also apply in these days for work, with little success thus far. But it's hard to be glum in Four Oaks. It's not Aleppo, Kabul, or Baghdad.

I ache from playing badminton, I'm tired because your sleeping has been rather erratic these past few nights, my lazy left eye droops, it could soon be sitting with my nostril. You weep downstairs, held by your Ma, she'll be whistling, or whispering German to you, I expect.

There is a photo of me and your Ma in Venice, at the central square. I see my hair, too short, and your Ma's left knee jutting outwards, as she poses for the picture, no doubt taken by another tourist, who today could feasibly be dead or alive, in Monaco or Mongolia. We stayed in

Treviso, a town nearby, a place I could live in. Endless pasta and gliding swans to glance at, during slow and rambling hand-in-hand walks, up the twisty river. There's a photo of your Grandparents in Shanghai, a palm tree on my Dad's T-shirt. Another tourist took that photo too, and he or she is conceivably in Lima or Lesotho. There's a photo of just me, sitting on a wall in Lanzarote, about to climb a mountain on Christmas day. A few days before, I bought a Spanish fan, for a woman who was, and is, not your Ma. Before I went to Cambodia, and my universe improved. The fan got lost one rainy Birmingham night, but the mountain was climbed well, by a man in cheap trainers and beige shorts. There's a photo of me and your Ma, on a beach somewhere, she clings to me, like a koala, from behind. She has bright red toe-nails, and I am slim, skinny, and tanned. And I don't know where it is. Me and a cousin and your Ma dancing somewhere, my Ma with a friend at a wedding, my Dad in a race car, plus black and white moments too. Cheesy smiles.

I wish I had had a camera with me when we took you swimming recently. In Frankfurt, and then Bad Steben. You floated, with a little help, slapped the water, and didn't seem to mind at all when it (rather nastily) went in your face. In a 'waterproof' nappy. You didn't even cling to us, let alone scream or wail. You're a dolphin. You even fell asleep at one point. The back of your hair, like Ophelia's, wet and slipping under, but your face untouched, immune to the water, your eyes dimmed, and then shut, eyelashes long and dry, and as delicate as a cherub's sigh. What baby sleeps in the water? Seriously? Well, I know one, and it happens to be you, you, you. You giggled when I slapped my face into the water and made a 'funny noise'. Yes, you said with your turquoise-sky eyes, that's my Dadda, and he's alright. I have rarely been happier. Bad Steben, and its thermal swimming baths don't get the acclaim of New York in spring or The Alps in winter, but I'd have to say that I prefer it. It's where your Ma is from, and it's wet, and warm, and now you like it too.

Sing a holy song
For today, the leaves are alive
And graceful ponies, four
Greeted their compadre, five

Clap a crusty tired hand
For every belly is not full
So be grateful, usurper
For some have a plate of null

Whistle a jaunty tune
When you rustle through the bushes
For fortune's finger is fickle
And she kisses all she touches

Smile a stupid bleeding grin
While you can, be willing and able
There's gold in teeth and silver in hair
And frequently food at the table.

When memories are put to sleep, and couples disperse, and destroy what they love most, be brave, little one. Raise your proud head, and smile at the many clouds. Whether in Four Oaks or The Philippines, on short or long journeys, give a thought to the forgetful and the freezing. This is my advice from twenty-twenty; discard your Dadda's poetry, and advice, but always take plenty of pictures.

Thirteen

I walked up and down this damned high street, just, at least four times. Once to get to the café I wanted to go to, but it was too busy. The second time was back to where I started because there was nothing else suitable. The third time was back to the 'original café', still too busy, and I felt utterly foolish for thinking that it would have emptied in ten or so minutes. The fourth time was back to where I started, again, to this insipid place, where I write now. The waitress seems Turkish or Turkish-German, she has a lovely smile and is overweight. You are half a year old tomorrow. Happy kind-of birthday. She just brought me a drink and now her smile has vanished. Then she came back to ask if I wanted to eat something. "Nein danke" I said. I'll stick with my non-alcohol beer. It's okay. I walked past the Irish pub earlier, and I fantasized about going in there and drinking four or five pints of Guinness, as was my habit, not long ago in Birmingham (I think this was on the third of my four walks). I changed my mind halfway to the door and decided to just have a non-alcohol beer instead. The Irish pub was closed anyway. It has been more than a year and a half now, being completely alcohol-free, and still every day, I grapple with the bottle, and I alone understand my Sisyphean labours. It's Sunday today, and that means that all the shops are closed, only the cafés and restaurants are open. The teenagers and the old couples and the teenaged couples stroll around smiling. And why shouldn't they? It may be chilly, bun the sun is out, and people should probably try to be happy. This is Bayreuth, city of your Ma's and my 'second wedding'. It's famous for Wagner, who was a shite as a human being, and, in my mind, an overrated composer. But people who know an awful lot more about these things, well, they call him a genius, and people come from all over the world to listen to his operas here. There are lots of little statues here, of him, dotted all around this high street. And all of them depict a pro-Nazi person. These things should be said, shouldn't they? But hey, little one, tomorrow, tomorrow…

Six months old tomorrow, and a few days ago, you crawled, really crawled, not just kind-of rolling around and somehow getting somewhere. No. Really crawled. Both hands flat, bum up, feet wiggling, and then, the acceleration, the movement. You are on video doing it, your face was determined (like Hillary charging up the mountain, leaving Sherpa Tenzing Norgay behind, racing to the summit). No more rolling places now, your efficient German side will not allow such a waste of valuable movement and motion.

Six months old tomorrow, but today two large women with green hair and three children just walked in. The women have nose-rings. To be brutally honest, I do hope that you don't have one attached to you as you read this. But who in the hell am I to try and do anything about it if you have?

Six months old tomorrow, so we should make you half of a cake. You eat now too, by the way. Mushy food, pulverised to a mash, healthy and wholesome. Sometimes I feed it to you, and sometimes your Ma does, or I try to hold your hands and then she feeds you. Or, you sit on my lap and she feeds you. So far, you've had zucchini, carrots, pumpkin, broccoli, and butter-nut squash (and a tiny piece of Opa's potato dumpling, which you pulled a lovely face at). And so far, apart from the target, your mouth, the grub has also been on your chin, on both cheeks, on your nose, up your nose, around your nose, under both eyes, and even on your neck, and of course, splattered Pollock style, the fingers and hands. I don't know if the large variety of places where the food goes is because of your eating, or our feeding. Needless to say, the neck time was one of my own efforts.

Six months old tomorrow, and humour masks the clown's woe, disguises his tears and puts a distance between turmoil and smiles. This morning, you fell out of the bed. You rolled slightly to the right, and then like a cat, landed on all four limbs. Then cried, just a little. It was my fault. I felt dreadful. The results could have been catastrophic, and not even this harlequin clown could then have attempted even a micro-second of happiness or humour, if his tiny daughter had hurt herself. No. If *his* negligence had caused her to be injured. In Oma's bedroom, which we currently sleep in, you in your Ma's old cot, and me and her squashed and squeezed in together in the single bed. You woke at nine which meant we did too. I had to change your nappy. I was half asleep. No. Excuses won't cut it. I put down the towel, then the nappy bag thing. Pyjamas off, 'body' undone, nappy off, and then vast amounts of pumpkin squashed into poo shit, and I marvelled at it and then said that we could mention it to the doctor on Monday. Then I actually tried to show the (full) nappy to your Ma. Your poor sleep-deprived, tired, nursing Ma, who, probably, just wanted to catch some sleep before the day began, and who almost certainly didn't want to look at a nappy full of pumpkin shite. Then, you rolled. You fell to the floor. I am lucky. I am foolish. Again, I questioned myself, my responsibilities to you. And if this vapid testimony is ever held against me, then so be it.

Six months old tomorrow, but today three Turkish or Turkish-German kids are being marched out of here by their mother, who, I think, works here. The waitress brings me another drink, and looks over these pages I've scrawled on. But no comment, other than "Bitte schön". She doesn't know that I've immortalized her in print, her smile and her heftiness. Monstrous of me, maybe. But who else will write about her, or even to her? Maybe multitudes for all this pea-brained man knows.

Six months old tomorrow, and before my eyes you have turned from a baby into an infant. You crawl now, you eat now, you will speak soon, you will walk soon, you will have many opinions about many subjects. You will read soon, you will go to kindergarten, school, college, university, order food and drink on your own, and not need my clumsy hands to help you. You won't need me for anything, one day soon. I am in a café. You are with your Ma.

Six months old tomorrow, and you had a fever a few days ago, you poor little bugger. A sweaty forehead, and a high, too high, temperature, that scared your Ma, and caused me to sweat a bit too. At first, I gormlessly, thought it was because you were wearing too many clothes, wrapped up too much to combat this harsh German winter. But no, you were quite ill, but apart from your forehead, you hardly showed it. No tears, no screams, not even a baby's sigh, only heard in heaven. So I came out with claptrap, like "No, I think she's fine. I think she could be wearing too many clothes. I think she will be fine after a good sleep. I think she will be alright tomorrow." I think I really should think twice, or think again, or think a little smarter, huh?

Six months old tomorrow, and then we go to Berlin on Wednesday. For five and a half weeks. Your second time, the capital is calling again. Your Ma will do a test, to maybe work for the E.U. in the future. I will do my teaching. We will explore, we shall show you the old and cold metropolis. East and west in unison again. Your Ma will also work for a month, for the U.N. again, so that means that most of the time, you will be in my butter-fingers. What should I show you?

Six months old tomorrow, but today we are in Bayreuth, and old people grimace as they pass by my window here. Dads in woolly hats chase their kinder, cappuccino machines whirr and buzz, bikes wheel past, Sunday goes on, hands in pockets and brows furrowed, and life's tyres gain more tread, scarves are wound around and around, shop windows promise love and excitement, glamour, and deliver only tacky crappy goods, made in sweatshops, in countries whose names they can't pronounce, let alone have been to. Some men wear white jeans, and some men are losing their hair, some men are bad and some men are good and some take their eyes off their kids and let bad things happen, and Germans and Turks and German-Turks walk past Wagner statues and everyone seems to care way too much about their phones, and not enough about important things, and people eat too much in the west, and don't let others eat, and there are more slaves in the world today than in any point in history, and that's a fact, and you are six months old tomorrow, so don't worry about it either.

Six months old tomorrow. In Germany, in a 'onesie', in Bayreuth, and then in Naila, in Oma's apartment, in your cot, in a sleeping bag, in the brown and green eyes of your parents. In the warmth, and in your belly, there will be milk and pumpkin mash. And in your bed, in your head, you will be thinking great, wonderful things. But in fact, you won't give two zucchini-green, carrot-orange shits, about the fact, that you, my little cherub, will be six months old. Tomorrow.

Fourteen

Too long, little one. Too long again since I last wrote to you. Here we are again, back in Berlin, your second time in this great city. I don't have to search far and wide for answers to my question, which is 'Why am I not writing to my daughter more often?'. Two answers are right in front of me, on this table. The first is a small round turquoise-coloured bowl, with mashed-up carrot inside. Your leftovers from lunch. The day starts with changing your nappy, then we feed you breakfast, usually banana, then change your nappy again, as by that point, usually, a small pebble of poo has been deposited, and tucked away in your nappy. Then I change your clothes, you wriggle and roll on the bed, and try to touch, or eat, your ten toes, and try to grab the nappies, or the wet wipes. Or anything in the vicinity that takes your fancy. Then we try to eat, but you crawl, you wail, and head towards the nearest sharp or hard object, as this always seems to be your sworn mission, when placed down by us. So we pick you up, talk to you, kiss your little round belly. In the meantime, there is washing up to be done, clothes to wash, vacuuming etcetera. Then your Ma works for one or two hours, and I half play with you, and half read or look at my phone. Then it's time for my work. Which is the second answer. An A4-sized notepad is next to the discarded mushy grub. In it, contains all of my work. A Saudi student, a Turkish professor of philosophy, a Brazilian film producer, a Vietnamese I.T. lady, young and old Chinese students, a Japanese surgeon, and today, there was an autistic boy, also Saudi Arabian. Is it even important that he is autistic? Should I even describe him as that? Do I take away his complexity as a human being with this simplistic adjective? Maybe.

And again, I tell you about me. Let us talk about the world instead, not just the tiny world in my computer, or on these Berlin streets. Did I even tell you about President Trump or Prime Minister Boris or Chancellor Angela? No. There is also a virus which is killing people around the world, at the moment, these past three months, it's called the coronavirus. Seems like everyone did their best to ignore it, until it was too late, and banged on their front door. That's what people are talking about. The Chinese are kept indoors, quarantined, worried, confused, containing, or not containing their fear. And here, they try not to be racist. 'I am not a virus', as the campaign says. I think of racism now. It's thoroughly despicable and as with most dreadful things, it will no doubt be continuing into your formative and even later years. Muslims are terrorists, black people are drug dealers, Chinese people are a virus, white people rule the world. It's so easy, this racism, no wonder so many seem to like it. Adjectives do simplify. And us English, we're tea-drinking drunks, and Germans, well, they are all efficient sausage munchers. And you, little Roman, you're pizza, pasta, Mamma-mia. This is how a lot of people still think in 2020, and it's so abysmal, isn't it? And this, I come to realize, is why I don't tell you much about the world. But is a Dadda who keeps his child in the dark a good Dadda? Maybe in a year or two, I'll tell you about genocides in the past and in the present. You will certainly know by now, not so little one, reading *now*. And for this, and for all of the atrocious crap you will find out about, I am occasionally sorry that this is the world we have brought you into. This maelstrom of sadness.

It's always close to home. Okay, maybe not in Four Oaks, Naila, or Rehau. But in Berlin, certainly. They say that one in three women were raped after the Soviet soldiers 'liberated' the city. But I wander down the streets today and see happy families, hipsters, a grand functioning city, sehr international, on the go, on the move, going jogging, going to work, crowding the S-bahn, racing up and down the stairs of the U-bahn, eating, drinking. And these people too, must forget the past, in order to move on, in order to put food on the table. Here in Prenzlauer Berg I am today, in the north. I also lived in Pankow in the north of the city, Charlottenburg in the west for one month, Lichtenberg in the east (with your Ma) for over a year, and last week we were staying in Neukölln, in the south of the city. Berlin is important to our story, the tale of the three of us. Your parents' first home together. The apartment was nice and big, but the street was old and it always seemed cold. The neighbours were loud and weird, the supermarket was cheap, the U-bahn station down the road was vast and smelt quite strange. But in that apartment we lived and loved and, ate and drank and played with Pepper. And hey, good days were many and bad days were few.

You are out with your Ma (as you often are when I finally shake the rust off my biro and get around to scribbling lines to you). We are staying in an apartment of a good friend of your Ma's, while she is away, working in Colombia. We also expect our own visitors soon, Grandparents (all four of them, plus Caro) will descend on us from England and Germany. Plus, Uncle Lennie, your Great Uncle. A Great uncle of mine was killed in the war, by Germans, as part of his paratrooper regiment. Your Great Uncle is visiting Berlin to see family, and to do some sightseeing. This must be progress, I think. So, don't let me paint the whole world as hopeless, and us as helpless, we certainly are not. There is progress. And there should be even more by the time you are my age. There is always hope.

I write, and have written, poetry. This, you know. Once upon a time, I once wrote in a notebook I had taken from my employees, a line from a poem. 'There's always hope, that's how we cope'. This line is of course a turgid poetic line, like the well intentioned efforts of a ten-year-old, forced to write a poem in English class, and trying desperately to think of a word to rhyme with 'hope'. "Pope, nope, dope, soap, elope" he or she says out loud until he or she settles on 'cope'. Please don't read my notebooks from around this time. If you think this is bad...

But hey baby, time's a wastin', it will soon be time to pack up and leave again, and cling onto your gypsy parents, as we trek onwards. It won't be Rwanda, I can tell you that. It won't be Antartica either, but with your parents, you never know. So here is where it could be, soon, after Berlin, in two or three weeks from now. So soon that the next chapter of this odyssey could be written there. Tunis in Tunisia or Lima in Peru. These are the options, the two choices. As random as if we had spun a globe, all lit up and pretty, closed our eyes, and put two fingers on two countries. Tunisia has beaches, but Peru has Paddington Bear and Macchu Picchu. And hopefully not the coronavirus. It would be quite nice if that didn't kill me any day soon, I do think about that. I mean, who would teach M____ the months of the year? It aint easy, I can tell you. Who would teach I_____ idioms? P____ pronunciation? G_____ new grammar? F_____ future tenses? And who would do farting and burping noises on your neck and belly, to make you squeal and giggle and chuckle? Well, I suppose your Ma could, but *I* want to do it.

Who will tell you that North Korea and Cuba are the only two countries on earth where you can't buy Coca-Cola? Who will tell you that the hottest chilli pepper in the world can actually kill you? (And so, realistically, you should probably avoid it and just have a different chilli instead). Who's going to tell you that The Canary Islands are named after dogs (and not, you know, canaries). Did you know that four babies are born every second? Now you do. Did you know that I cried when *you* were born? Not straight after, but when I summoned up the courage to touch a little hand. You know that too, now. And there are so many people alive in 2020, that this is actually seven percent of all of the folks who have ever lived. And you are one of them. It's up to one hundred and eight billion now, since we first hit the scene. And Muhammad is the most popular boy's name. But we would have preferred Samuel if you were to have been a boy. And I guess, by now, you know that your Father likes facts and figures. But did I tell you yet that he had cancer once? Maybe I did, and I've forgotten. Another fact is that even with just the one testicle, I can help to make a baby.

The carrots, blended and boiled, are getting cold. The notepad is losing work pages and gaining writing pages. Six cushions sit on the floor, in a largely futile attempt to stop you from escaping from your play area. Ma's pilates mat is next to her rucksack, which is next to my shoulder bag. The light is on, but I don't need it on. I need to shave and shower. I forgot to make myself a coffee. This is *my* world now.

Your Ma feeds you milk, she works a few hours per day, she sees her friends, calls her friends, messages with her

Ma, reads a book about starving people, makes food for you, and occasionally uses the pilates mat. This is *her* world now.

You eat banana for breakfast, vegetables for lunch, and porridge for dinner, then you crap it all out in weird shapes and colours. You chew on a five-sided blue plastic star, you sleep a little, you cry a little, you don't really crawl properly yet, but you do drag yourself along. You love to laugh, and I think you love your Ma and me too. This is *your* world.

These last two things make my world an incredible one.

And hey, call me an optimist, or maybe just a crap writer, but there is this too:
There's always hope
That's how we cope.

Fifteen

You can ask any person, right now, in the whole sodding big wide world, this question: "How are things where you are?", and they will know exactly what you mean. People are comparing these days to World War Two, and to be fair, it does seem like there are very limited comparison points. This year is the year that you will turn one year old, but to most people, looking back, this will be the year that the coronavirus took hold of our flimsy planet. From Taiwan to Timbuktu to Boston to Botswana, they will all frown and say "Not so good". The lucky ones, like us, will say "Well, the shops and restaurants are closed, and we don't go out much at all, but we can go to the supermarket, and get some exercise, and we work from home". This must be the best possible answer, that the uninfected can reply with. Even the term 'the uninfected' seems to me like a term from a zombie horror film, and not something a real-life person can relate to. Well, real life is still real, but now it is all *too* real. The unaware can say "Well, I have a cough, but hopefully it is nothing more than that...". The grieving say "Unfortunately my Mum/Dad/etcetera passed away this week/this month". These are the only three available answers, really, the big question. The only people who are allowed to not reply, are those, who (as Jack Kerouac wrote) are 'safe in heaven, dead'.

I must tell you these terrible things, as it seems terrible to not mention them. Six hundred and eighty-three people died, on Friday, in the U.K. alone. A similar number in

Spain, in Italy, even more in the U.S. Everywhere is affected. Here in Germany, the cases are up, but the deaths are down. Thank heaven for small mercies.

It seems the language of god and religion is never far away, in these trying days.

The last time that your Ma and I had our ongoing debate about Him (or the lack of him) was on Friday. While my country was turning exhibition centres into makeshift hospitals, we took the train to see your uncle. Strolling through the streets, in the sun, in a haze of nonchalance, a fugue state of denial. We even had a barbecue. In this city, Nuremburg, in the past, bombs by the thousands fell. Seventy-five years ago, I'm sure they were not barbecuing. So thank heaven too, for burnt feta and sub-standard halloumi. Details need not be mentioned, especially not in this time, until we said our 'Tschüss's' and our 'Bis Balds'. Then it happened. Then, I carried you, and your Ma carried a basket of laundry. We walked towards the steep and narrow staircase. Bang. Crash. Wallop. Swearing and Oh God, Oh God, Oh God. I ran down the stairs, and put you in your new push-chair. You seemed unaware. Unaware of the fact that your Ma had just fallen down the stairs. Face-first. Not one or two steps. More. More like eight or nine or more. The moment, the micro-second, was a blur, it always is, of movement and sound. The moments after, we remember, I think. Like the neighbour asking us if we were okay. "Nein!" I said "Meine Frau… erm…", then I did the universal sign for 'fell', with my hand. Then, in a jumbled mix of Germ-glish "It's okay. Kein problem". I lied, the problem at that very moment was not small, or to be brushed off. In fact, at that precise moment, if truth be told, I would have been ecstatic if it was 'only a sprained ankle, or cuts and bruises, or even some sort of twisted ligament. But what I really thought was that it was a broken leg, or arm, or worse. From what I saw, the plummeting, I thought broken neck, or worse... Wheelchairs and hospitals, and... nothing good in the foreseeable future. Our future. The three of us. Your uncle came to see what had happened, your Ma shouted him. There were bruises, a little blood, but every limb was intact and moving. It seemed unreal, then I wasn't thinking 'lucky escape', 'thank god' etcetera, I was thinking 'No, it's *too* lucky. Not like when I fell in Paris, or when you rolled off the bed. No. I expected a broken limb this time. *Minimum*. What I got was your uncle picking up the laundry, and your Ma cracking jokes about ripping her jeans. I remained apoplectic, speechless, very dumb, or sweary, depending on my oscillating mood, at the moment. She stood up. Then you cried and I said "It's okay. Mama tried to jump down the stairs instead of walking down them". It was not funny. And then less than ten seconds later, we were bickering. About lightbulbs. You don't need every little detail. Only this, you should know, the old grim reaper is too busy, at the moment, he doesn't want to be pratting around on staircases, just waiting. And you can call that grim or you can call it black humour or even a miracle, like your Ma did at the time. We bickered about that too, straight after. Only later, when we had really caught our breath, when we put cold pressure on the bumps, on the blood, on the bruising, when I looked up at the sky. Which still, to me, is clouds, but which to your Ma is heaven, only then did we hug, and speak kind slow words to one another. Only then...

And now. Now, she is cutting up a sweet potato for you. You are valiantly attempting to climb out of the chair that is pulled up to the table in the kitchen. I only scribble with a crap pen, wearing a creased mustard-coloured shirt, and feel quite self-conscious while I write these words, now. Now we have to shout a little at you, and we tell ourselves that it is for your own good. You throw a giraffe on the floor, I pick it up, same again, I shouldn't keep picking it up. I give you a little penguin, a little yellow car, fall, fall, falling away, they all go, onto the kitchen floor. It's nice to write to you again, so you can perhaps read these words in the future. But in the present, you are hungry, and agitated, and too many of 'my people' are dying, and all I'm doing is teaching phrasal verbs and pointless idioms to people with a bit too much time on their hands. This is how it feels, sometimes. "Down, down, down!" I shout. Your little face looks disappointed.

Break. Must see parents...

We skyped. They seemed okay.

This is my paradox. My first-world problem, or one of them. What I want to do is write to you. But I can't. Because of you. No, that's not entirely fair. And it is only partly true. I'm working more too. This lockdown is worldwide, so people have to stay at home. So, what do they get up to while they do? Well, mostly the world is watching the news, and buying toilet paper in ginormous quantities, in a futile attempt to try and feel like they are not entirely powerless (I am pleased to report that in our household, the bog-roll buying is kept to a completely normal level). And the kids play video games, and stare at their phones, whilst the parents watch television, and stare at *their* phones. But some people actually do take the time to be creative and learn (I am not one of these people), like, learn or improve another language for example. And that's where I come in.

My other problem, that is a nice problem to have, is me. Or me and you. Your Ma told me that I 'huff and puff' with you. And that I have less patience with you than she does. Maybe this is true, and this thought is rather sad. I explain my defence thus: I huff and puff because I'm not happy when you're not happy. For example, when I try to change your nappy, and you try to grab the wet-wipes packet (you bloody love that wet-wipes packet, just saying), or when we try to feed you, and you grab the food, or the food jar, or stand up in the chair, or don't open your mouth at all, or when you… Well, you get the picture. Sorry. This alleged project of mine should celebrate you and not bitch about you. And I'm sorry for when I huff and puff. I'm sorry. Stop.

We can't go to Tunis, because we can't fly anywhere. We can't go to Peru, because they want someone else (someone who is not your Ma). We can't fly to England, we can't go to Rome, we can't even see your Oma for Easter in Naila. But we can see your first teeth coming through, slowly but surely (and painfully too, for you, I fear), and we can see you standing up in the play-pen, your feet tentatively step-stepping, as your tiny fingers grasp the wooden bars. We hear the tap-tapping of those teeth on the plastic cup that you drink water from. We hear you laugh, we see you grow. We can see 'old' photos of you (not yet eight months old) of you, and we sweetly lament 'She's not our baby anymore. She's an… an infant'. And we can take you to some places, and show you chickens, and pigeons, and push your pushchair in the direction of ducks in the park. The very same place where the Nazis held their rallies, now you chuckle at the ducks. Those silly little ducks quack-quacking. We're here in this big old Russian fusty apartment, the three of us. Laughter echoes around the furniture-less empty rooms, and reverberates off the walls, and hopefully, into our memories.

Face-first your poor wee head went into the wooden bars, you had crawled over to see what I was writing. I said "You don't get to read this for another seventeen years or so". You laughed, hopped on one foot. You are wearing a red dress, and you have a lady-bird hair-clip keeping your fair-haired parting in one place. Your blue eyes shine in the late evening sun. The sun in Bavaria warms its cold breezes, and keeps the rustling trees smiling.

We can't do this or that. We can do this or that. But then, isn't that always the way?

Grandparents cannot see their grandchildren, instead they skype. Or here, they throw sweets from their apartment balconies, four stories down, into the excited clutching hands of their progenies progeny. I see my parents only on a screen. You get to see yours, pretty much, twenty-four seven. Mine were in Berlin for a week, but they had big troubles trying to get back home. Several flights cancelled, and an unexpected and unwanted overnight stay in Dusseldorf too. My Dad is seventy, and yours is thirty-eight, right now, while he lies on the floor and writes this, to you. How many more years will I be here to worry about you? How much worry will you give me?

People are dying, and will die, and more tomorrow, and the days after. I know our 'problems' in this echoing old flat are utterly minuscule, I tell myself this, I should. Until bigger ones come, until the falls are not being brushed off, and joked about immediately afterwards. Until we are the ones calling ambulances, until we are the unfortunates, with the troubled eyes and the sad words. Until we are the sick, the ill, the dying, we will remain. The world today can sometimes resemble a horror movie, both before and after this virus. But still I remain a happy fool, on the floor with small small problems. And your hair is in your eyes, and drool is falling down your mouth, and the lady-bird is still in your hair, and the red dress is not yet stained, and your white tights look brand new, and while you bounce up from every fall, and while the bumps are minimal, while the smile stays in your eyes, I will teach and write and try to be a Father. To you, Emily Salome' Colbourne. You should know I really mean it when the middle name is included.

It feels like the end
But it could be the beginning
And all the stars still shine
When the lamp-post lights go off.

Sixteen

Where are we, now? I hear you ask.
Röthenbach.
Röthenbach?

Röthenbach, yes. And where is that? Where was I when I was almost nine months old? Well, I shall tell you.

Y____ Y_____ is twenty-six years old. He has a kind face, darting eyes, and a half-hearted attempt at a beard. He likes football, and he works for an oil company. He is from Kagoshima in the south of Japan, he has just returned from a spell in Darwin in Australia, to live in Tokyo again. I see him on a screen once a week, for thirty minutes. We chat and I correct his mistakes. My relationship to him is teacher to student, with slight undertones of matey friendship. It's fair to say that I like him, he seems like a nice bloke, a good guy. If they have Mother's Day in Japan, it's safe to say that he remembers to send his Ma some nice flowers. In this month, in this year, in this town, I see him on our Fujitsu laptop. There is nothing especially remarkable about him, as far as I can gather.

This morning, I woke up at approximately eight o'clock, which was later than in recent days. The first thing I see is you, not your Ma. The first thing I hear is you, crying and shouting. Sleep to you is a concept not yet fully comprehended. Milk to you is a want, a great need, to which you are its disciple. Your Ma and me lay in bed, while you climbed on us, trying to ascend the headboard. On this headboard, there are faux-diamonds attached. You scratch the headboard with your fledgling nails, and seem content when you are standing up, clutching it. Afterwards, we climb the stairs together, the three of us, around a bend, to the kitchen. We make and eat breakfast together, a family. Cereal for me and your Ma, and porridge and banana for you. My nickname is Schnupp-schnupp, your nickname is Nuk-nuk, and your Ma's is Flup-flup. I don't think that I understand completely the origins of these names. I am big hiiid, you are micro hiiid, and your Ma is medium hiiid. Hiiid means head. This much, I do know.

Not long after breakfast, I traipse downstairs, and turn on the computer. The password is awkward. A picture of you then appears, from when you were three or four months old. It appears 'the wrong way around', and I usually crane my head sideways so that I can look at it better. You are smiling, quite enigmatically. I log onto my employer's website, and then prepare my 'reservation lessons' (including Y____, he is easy to prepare). Just before it is time to start work, I return upstairs and kiss you and your Ma. She always says "Good luck", but this morning she almost forgot.

I talk to people for a living. Correct them, help them, remind them about using the correct tense, and to use plurals in the right way. I always introduce myself to new students, like this:
'Hi. My name's James (pause). I am from England (pause), but (pause) I live in Germany'. I feel that this is a good way to say hello, after they have done likewise. Sometimes, I say the south of Germany, sometimes I say Bavaria. But few seem to know Bavaria. In which case, I say "close to Munich". We don't live near Munich at all,

but the options are rather limited in this endeavour. Maybe then, some will say something like 'Ahh, Bayern Munich, the football team'. This makes life easy because I can then say something like 'Yes Munich, I live in Bayern, close to Munich'. This establishes common knowledge and a little common ground, which, it seems to me, is quite an essential aspect of teaching a foreign language. If they've never heard of Bayern Munich, I'll say 'Yeah, it's in the south'. 'Okay', they'll then say, perhaps losing interest, and wondering why the frigging hell they even bothered calling me in the first place. If they don't grasp the idea of 'south' (or if they pretend to grasp it), as opposed to the idea of 'north', then I'm pretty sure that the next thirty or so minutes will potentially be quite difficult.

I never say I live in Röthenbach. Which is the truth.

It is close to Nuremburg. It's Frankonia. It's Bavaria. It's Germany (some kids don't even know Europe, by the way). It's in the countryside, this temporary home of ours. To the left is forest, to the right is forest, behind us, well, there is a big forest. I feel like frigging Robin Hood. In front, there is a train station, where we take the choo-choo to Nuremburg. Next to the train station, I think there is a forest.

And we walk, oh how we walk, in these virus days. With a mask in my back pocket, and a flat wallet in my left. With you in your trusty blue Swedish carrier, or pushing the pushchair, with you strapped in, glaring at the sun's rays, and the neat gardens, and the clean streets, and the intact pavements. You are, technically, a Roman, and so therefore must feel like a real foreigner here, especially in this last regard, as the roads and pavements in your birth city are beyond useless. There are two supermarkets, an ice-cream place or two, and there are two banks. Forty minutes down the road, there's a pretty city, medieval and modern at the same time. This is called Lauf. But we live in Rothenbach, with a middle-aged lady living downstairs, who talks on the phone a lot, and who lives within a one-minute walk away from her ex-husband. We met him, he smelt a little sweaty, but he is friendly and beardy. He's not great at carrying sofas, but hey, you can't have everything.

I am upstairs-upstairs now, at the kitchen table, looking at roses, and the washing up, and the mass of papers and various objects that sit on the table. I think you've gone to Lauf.

The next time I write, we could be in Tunis. In Tunisia, in Africa, in only three-weeks-time. It's possible. But I think I've told you that before, haven't I? Some 'educated people' must have ball-bags for brains and the communicative skills of deaf and dumb badgers. I'd like to live in Tunis, for a few months or more, if only a few cretinous buffoons could pull their fingers out of their…

Speaking of which… you had diarrhoea dropping from yours. Waves and currents of green and brown shite, flowing through the nappies, and into my hands. The filled nappies then filled the bags, which we keep in the bathroom. The window opening is very minimal (and the sink is much too close to the mirror over it, so you have to put your head right under it too much). We must hold our breath when we open and close the bag. There was a little blood in your nappy two weeks ago.

The docs looked at it. And at you. And proclaimed all okay. "Don't worry. It will be alright. If she's drinking? Yes? Then that's fine. If she seems alright, then that's fine" (all this in German of course, so my translation may be less than pristine). But, just to be safe, they tested your shite, had a good look at it. Then they called us and said "Salmonella".

Little micro-hiiids like you can die from that, and have died from that, in fact. We don't know where you got it from. About this whole crappy episode, I feel terrible, useless, dim, and about one thousand other unpleasant adjectives. But you've always seemed alright, so that's fine. But is it fine? Are you alright? Tell me. In English, please.

Your English Grandparents aren't going out much at all at the moment, for fear of covid, which means illness, which could mean rolling a seven, which means not seeing me or you ever again, probably. Your German Grandparents seem okay. Oma is happy with her new job, while Opa plays his tuba around Rehau (another small Frankonian-Bavarian-German town). So don't worry. Looking back on these days, you might see them as 'The Coronavirus days, when I was a baby'. But it's all just dust swept under the rug, and we do try to keep our fragile smiles.

What you should see, or know, is this. An email from your Ma to my Ma and Pa, it contains a video. It's you, laughing, and that is about it, really. But then, that is more than enough. I'm playing it now, it's only sixteen seconds long. We've sent it to a few countries by now, to our friends and family. Last night I told you that you are so special, you even make people smile and be happy, just by laughing. It's my mission to make you laugh. Putting a little toy llama on my head will do it, sliding a little toy penguin on the table will do it, imitating the odd way you drink will do it, jumping up and down whilst pulling faces will sometimes do it, biting your belly will definitely do the trick. Your laugh is incredible and better than just about anything else you or I care to mention. Watch the video if you don't believe me. I'm watching it again now…

Twenty-eight thousand dead in Britain now, from the virus. A national tragedy, a national outrage, people are dead, or dying, or hiding in their homes. They don't have much time to be angry, but I do, and I am. I'm glad we're in Germany, safe in this town, where the people in charge do seem to have more than a vague idea about what to do about the situation. You've got a German passport. Be glad for that. A kinderreisepass. It's not North Korean or Somalian or Congolese. You are not suffering or starving. You are laughing. So thank the dear old clouds for me, and thank god, for your Ma.

You will probably never meet my ex-wife, or my birth Mother. Just facts. The reasons are various and many. Stories, perhaps, for other days. These two important women…

What one said goodbye to
The other will never have
And moments can come clear and true
But they'll never be as blue
As that blue.

When I say goodbye to you, you come back. And music like that
Is pink and yellow and green and gold. And can never ever get old
When I say goodbye to you, you wear a smile. And while I'll be waiting, a short lucky time. I know that I'm
Not going back to her.
Or her.

Because one said goodbye
Then I said goodbye
The question is
Who will smile and who will cry?

I doubt Y__ Y_____ asks that question. He seems like a nice guy, so I hope he doesn't. And I hope you don't either.

Seventeen

Twenty minutes

You are asleep next to me, on the bed
I must be very quiet. Very, very quiet
Writing this now, with hurricanes swirling, significantly
Dangerously happy in my everything, almost.

The lady-bugs are going up and down, down and up, no frowns
On your dress and in my lungs, in my future, in my past
Right arm outstretched, left arm striking a heroic pose
Chasing birds and drinking milk and laughing
All in your sleep, all in your dreams, of strawberry chocolate lemonade

(We are still in Röthenbach. But Tunisia looks hopeful. Hamburg on Wednesday is certain, to see your Great-grandparents, and hopefully your dear sugar-sweet cousin. Rome is hopeful too. All is hopeful in a moment like this. Coronavirus, war in Yemen, war in the world, spread out across every continent, it all seems so far away today).

I told you about the birds
The colours and the shapes and the flies and the bees
I said 'Pink there, yellow there, red there, behind it blue
Wood and grass and green and trees'
I sang, you slept, I carried you in

It's Sunday. Still asleep. Banana almond, sweet potato, porridge dreams
Cats and pigeons and nanas and squirrels.

A day not to know the date
Or even think twice about the month
But remember it's Sunday. Sleeping schlafen müdes Mäuschen
Forget about spelling and grammar and the second conditional
On the condition that you remember this day
The lady bugs dancing, the hair in your eyes
The white tights a little too tight (you don't need shoes)
You don't need the owl suit, or the internet, or tears today
You're stirring, stirring, I'm afraid, I'm afraid you'll wake
With the pitter-patter of your Ma's feet, naked on the floorboards
Afraid more that you'll roll again, onto the floor, onto the boards
Water in the flowers, new blue socks on feet, your Ma slips by
Slips along the balcony, almost silently, almost gracefully, but
The door almost woke you

Putting socks away, that kind of day
Telling each other dreams, that
You can't remember. She said days should have tombstones, that
Dogs are unspectacular, sometimes without people, I disagree, I need
Books and paper and lady bugs on dresses, stripy, up and down
And if this is an interlude, then let it be a weekly one
And then five angels, can come, and have some
Yorkshire tea with us.

But we won't let them
Put too much sugar in.
We're sweet enough.
I'd say so.

Sucking your thumb now, I'm scared to move. Afraid
I'm scared a feckless boy will break your heart, some handsome bastard. Boy
Scared a nasty girl will make you cry, some pretty bastard. Girl
Scared some teacher will shout in your soul, an adult
(worst of all, me, worst of all, me, this bastard). Me.
Scared a car will come too close and scare you. You.
Scared a drop of water will drop on your head. Yours.
And scared still, you'll drop off this bed.
Scared volcanoes will spew disaster. Them.
Scared oceans will swallow you. Those.
Scared leaves will scratch your fingers when they fall. Them.
Scared people will die and then I'll cry and then you'll cry and then and then... Then.
Then you'll be alright because your Ma. Her.
She'll tell us not to be scared. Us.

But lady bugs are stronger than they seem
Even cotton ones from H&M
Somewhere in some town
On the third floor
Next to the men's section

And now you've woken up
And didn't fall off the bed
Hair in your eyes, confusion too
Grabbing this pen
Tiny wilful fist and fingers
So now I must turn off this writing

And turn on the task of being
Dadda, Dadda, Dadda, Dadda, Dadda, Dadda...

Eighteen

This table is unbelievably dirty, unbelievably full of things, unbelievably attached to my elbow, attached to my arm, to my shoulder, one hand is on my forehead, the other writes letters, which make words, which comprise of letters, which comprise of symbols, which seem to be known as the English language, of which I suppose I am, in some ways, a teacher of.

Owww says the broken thumb, which a man from Walsall broke when he pushed me in Wolverhampton, and then the next day I went to Birmingham, and it was my first wife's birthday, which is the same day as your Oma's, to Sutton Park too, in the usual place, and I went to a hospital, which is sometimes harshly known as No Hope Hospital, on account of it being less than perfect, I suppose. Then we split up just over a month later, I moved into my parents' house after spending two or three bizarre nights on the sofa, in the living room, where we laughed together about me sleeping on the sofa, because she said that she should instead of me, which for some reason, I don't remember, made us laugh, and it is this one thing that hurts my heart right now more than anything else, except for when you had a fever for two and a half days, and now you're standing and making noises, like a constipated monkey, but still the pens swap on account of this broken thumb, and not long after it was broken, life changed immeasurably, and so now, I tell you off for chewing on a plastic bin bag, which is sticking out of a drawer slightly. What would the man from Walsall say about that, or my first wife, wherever she is? They might say "That was all just a few sentences, but you can't write like Laszlo Krasznahorkai, who writes entire chapters or stories using only one sentence". But anyway, there will be more sentences. Now your Ma has asked me to vacuum...

Still this project is a secret to all but me, you, the man on the moon, and your Ma. Oh, and a Korean woman. I mentioned it to her once, she's the kind of kind person who you tell things to. I told her I had cancer once, and her face did a kind of concerned and caring look, which lasted for over eleven minutes. I would call that a sure sign of a caring person, wouldn't you? I haven't vacuumed yet. This table is so messy, so messy. There's a pen, a phone, a mug, another phone, a jar, a spoon, a tissue box, flowers, a glass, a notepad, vitamin drops for you, your Ma's sunglasses (it's raining now, so they are even more superfluous), a yellow car (a toy car, not a real one with an engine), and one piece of paper with a few sentences on it. I still haven't vacuumed. I've been listing...

My rebellion of writing and not vacuuming has been crushed insidiously, by me, after twelve long minutes. Like Spartacus, I martyred myself. In your city, they crucified him, and all his mates, along the Appian Way. In your city. You seem unsure about the vacuum, eyeing it suspiciously, contemptuously, not smiling or frowning, but quizzically, you ponder the vacuum's use, existence, and purpose. But you do like the button, that when pressed, hurries the long black lead back to its cushy home inside its plastic cave. I don't even really know how that function works, except that when you press the button, it does the thing. Life could be made up of universes, gods and solar systems, but it is also full of things like 'the cord retraction button' on a vacuum, and the strangely alluring smell of earwax. Or the pleasing-to-the-ear-noise of a biro's nib coming out. The most pleasing sound in this life, to me, is and will be forever, your laughter. But also too, as is the norm, I do hear cries, sobs, and various other moans and complaints. I offer to take you from your Ma, who says you are talkative. I can't concentrate, and surely she can't either, as you are crying for no apparent reason. But stopping now, equally mystifying. A large conundrum you are sometimes, micro-hiiid...

Of which I notice more, as I am now working only two hours per day, instead of three or four, because your Ma's contract has finally landed, or rather, crash-landed in our laps. So, I prepare more food, I feed you more, I chase after you, I change your clothes more, I change more nappies, I play with you on the floor, in the play-pen, on the sofa, on the bed. And I do try ever so hard to be utterly present in these moments. But I fail all too often, sometimes abysmally. As I also check BBC news, BBC sport, and boxing websites, on our landlady's wi-fi, and check my book to see how many pages are in the next chapter, I research the book itself, I do washing up, I dry cutlery, or dishes, or plates, or bowls, or whatever else, when I should *be with* you, one hundred percent. Still, your little blonde-brown ponytail jumps cheerfully around, as you crawl to the next thing you wish to climb up. Your feet scuttle you to the next toy to play with, guided by your minuscule hands, which shoot you off, to the next thing to put in your mouth, which will soon be welcoming more teeth, more trouble, more things in it which shouldn't really be in it. Protruding bin-bags for example...

Maybe I have told you this before, but your Ma has told me that these writings 'tend to be jumpy'. She means that they include many, many subjects or topics. And she's right, they do. I suppose it's because I don't write often enough to you, and so, each time I do sit down to scribble unintelligible ramblings to you, I have several worlds stored up in my pen, ready to pour out their oceans of ink. Even doing this now, this questionable endeavour which is sound-tracked by your shouts and warbles and ravings, it is stopping me from seeing you playing under the table, with a blue plastic ring, and climbing up chairs, and clambering up, up, up.

I wish you wouldn't rattle the glass door that divides the living room from the landing area. I wish you wouldn't climb up the wooden stairs which lead to the loft. I wish you wouldn't slip and bang your nose, and then collapse on your tiny bum, and then cry, cry, cry. I wish you wouldn't wheeze, it worries me. I wish you wouldn't wriggle when I change your nappy. Or wiggle when I hold you, or lick cupboards, or bite drawers, or kiss the oven. But most of all, I wish I could stop bloody worrying. If parenthood has a curse to make up for its many gifts, it is surely the curse of constant worry. I have it in a bad way, in the worst way. I don't want it, not at all, but I don't see a way of getting rid of it.

We've been leaving the tiny town of Rothenbach lately, a little. Via cars, trains, walks, wheeling a pushchair, driving a fire-breathing truck... Well, that's another story... I'm jumping... So let's jump then...

But before we do, let me tell you some more about your home here, for it is indeed that now, or so it seems to us. This is the place where we shout "Nuk-nuk!", and you come scrambling, crawling rapidly around the corner, where you open the door that leads to the fridge, but have not yet quite figure out how to open the fridge door, where you sleep in forests, while being pushed or carried, where you roll the four plastic rings (your favourite is the blue one), where you scratch the bed's head-board, where you follow the birds across the endless sky, with your great blue unknowing eyes, where you wait impatiently for the train, while your Ma and me wear masks over our faces, because we must, in these confusing corona/covid times. And it is where you look around Aldi with us, where you queue in Edeka, where you just shut your thumb in the door, still, still, still, trying to get to the bloody fridge. You'd think we never fed you. But there is a jar of sweet potato and fennel, mushed-up and half eaten, on the table, amongst everything else, which tells us otherwise.

I suppose the people here are generally okay, and the kids are surprisingly polite, always saying 'danke' when you let them past on their speeding bicycles, but yes, and again, the small town mentality does bother me a little. They know bread and coffee and sausages by the billion, but they also know staring at 'out of towners', like a bible-belting small town Arkansas hick, and frowning does seem to be quite a popular pastime here, as is order, and then more order for good measure. The right way is their way. All of which merely confirms unanimously that I am a big-city boy, home in Berlin and Rome, but rarely infused with wonder at trees or muddy paths. It takes all kinds of strange folks to make up this world, and it is wrong, entirely snobbish, futilely insensible, to look down one's oversized nose at a man or woman or boy or girl, with his or her nose in a bible instead of a Penguin Classic. I'll just be happy if you're reading at all, I suppose, whether it be a bible or a book by Balzac or Bulgakov.

Talking of small towns, we went to Quickborn quite recently, ostensibly to see your Great-Grandparents, one of whom is curly haired, sturdy as only a German Frau can be, certainly feisty in her eyes but frequently ill now, unfortunately. She is eighty years old, the Mother of your Ma's Ma. But she, bespectacled and warm, didn't want to see us. The reasons are numerous, and, I fear, all too complicated. The other is a little younger, limping, goatee-bearded like a younger man, proud of his garden, a simple man, but maybe a man with a past that is less than spotless with regards to his parenting. I do try not to judge him (believe it or not), or anyone really. I only hear stories, you see, fragments of memories, tales of confusion, from which we inevitably form our easy opinions. They are all we have to guide us sometimes, when we need a compass to explore the tangled knot of the past. Did he ever chase his daughter across the room while she screamed in sheer delight? I don't know. I doubt it, but doubt is neither here nor there when we want the facts, and when we try to separate them from their strange cousin, fiction. Did he blend various vegetables, and patiently feed them to his daughters? To his kinder? Or did he instead fall into the well-laid trap of impatience instead? As I do, as we all do, sometimes.

Instead, we saw your cousin. His sweet demeanour, his patience (far out-stripping us adults), his kindness, his joy, his soul, all remain intact, hopefully indestructible. He picked a daisy for you, and placed it carefully in your clutching hand. You smiled at him. I have no picture of this on my phone, but I must maintain the clarity of the memory that I keep now. This shining moment. His light hair in the sun, the rain come and gone, your blue, blue eyes with several eternities inside them, and smiles and smiles. That was life. And instead, also, we saw Hamburg, which is a fine and large watery city. But I prefer to instead remember a daisy in a child's hand sometimes...

The car ride to Quickborn was a precursor, a dress rehearsal for an even bigger trip, a marathon drive through countries, to your birthplace, ancient Rome. And this is where the fire-breathing dragon appears in the story...

The truck was long and black and had a tail-lift, which gave me not at all sweet memories of moving the blasted bastard things up and down ad-infinitum on day shifts, and occasional nightshifts at a blasted bastard paper company. We woke early and took a train or two to the rental company, a surprisingly friendly young Frau even hopped up and swept the back of the van for us. With our rubber straps, we hooked up our bags, and then... Drove, on and on. Your Ma, trucker-like, high up in the driver's seat, one beady eye on the road and the other on the route on her smartphone. Me, sleepy, excited just a little, definitely apprehensive, at the thought of twelve-plus hours of driving ahead of us. And you, strapped in tightly to the car seat, sucking a digit or two, or chewing on the straps of the seat, or mercifully entertaining yourself with whatever toy I had plonked in front of you. And on and on we went, past small towns, past Munich, speeding on and on, with thoughts of Rome, our destination, and our purpose, the storage company, plus nicer ones of friends and pizza and cacio 'e pepe. And then Austria. Sodding Austria. The army boys at the border perused our passports, and did let us pass, but they did ominously warn us that it was forbidden to stop in their little Österreich, corona-virus safety measures etc. And that was when the floodgates opened. Rivers of tiny tears dripping down your perky nose, and settling on your chin. You wanted to be fed, but we couldn't stop. Damn those infernal Austrians. And so, for one whole hour, as we traversed the mighty Austrian Alps, heading towards Northern Italy, the crappy pop-pap on the radio was drowned out by wails and woe-filled watery whines. Oh, how you cried. Continually. Continuously. Finally, finally, the next border came. Italy, blessed Italy. The chance to stop and feed you, to fill your little belly with as much milk as your heart desired. Somehow, the sacred law of Sods Law decreed that that was the moment for the floodgates to be closed, and for the waterworks to desist. The term 'Sods Law', I feel, should have a far stronger expletive attached to it, in my humble opinion. But we were in Italy, at last, in a big truck, with a fire-breathing dragon painted on it...

We stayed one night with a friendly family in Verona. Another early rise, and then further trucking, on to Roma. Where the parking was as inexplicable as always, and our fellow drivers as incomprehensible and impatient as ever they were. Finally, I had to save a space, waving on frustrated and angry drivers, wording silently to them 'No, sorry. I'm sorry'. Perhaps I should have done it in Italian. There, our friend met us, from the (aforementioned) bible-belt (where eggs are 'ayygs' and 'y'all' is a common word in the vernacular), kind as a cousin, she is, and as helpful as Hercules holding your suitcases. She showed us to our lodgings. Surprisingly tidy for a family with four bambinos...

Rome, in many ways, belongs to an earlier time in this here tome. So let us keep it brief. Suffice to say, there were good friends to see, gelato digested by the gallon, and ancient cobbled streets to stroll up and down, sun-drenched we were, but happy little campers, certainly. I mean, sure, your Ma did, technically, drive the truck into the ceiling of the storage company, causing several hundred euros worth of damage. But hey, you know, we had given them plenty of money (or rather, your Ma did), and hey, what's a little damaged property between friends (or customers and disgruntled men in a small office)? Yes, Rome was fine and we even found time to be literally caught slap-bang in the middle of a riot (your first one. I wonder how many you're up to now, as you read this…). Heavily armed police on one side, and angry far-right protestors on the other. And us, a pair of wallies, with a calm little thumb-sucker, in the middle.

Yes, we lifted many things, fifty boxes, a piano, a jigsaw or two, plus various other assorted objects, accrued by your dear Mother in her relatively short life. We lifted them all, from the lock-up, to the tail-lift, to the van. Then took them to another country, and then another country, then reversed the procedure, took them to the truck, to the tail-lift, to your Oma's staircase, all five floors of it. Thankfully, your uncle did assist in this most uncomfortable labour. All was good, all worked out (riots and ceilings aside). But let's just not pass through Austria again, anytime soon. Let's give it, say, another thirty years, minimum (you bawled down the Alps on the way back too…).

Only three nights we stayed in Rome, leaving swiftly on the Sunday, after church for your Ma, and the beach for me. How joyfully I rushed to the crowded beach, purchasing an overpriced sunbed, sprawling out on it, admiring the vast blue perfection, feasting my eyes on its salty miracle. Plenty of paprika Pringles swallowed down, I stripped to my holey boxer shorts, whipped them off as stealthily as I could (avoiding flashing one's genitals to my fellow beach-goers), swim-shorts on, and trotted, ultra-gleefully, to the gentle waves lapping the shore. Oh, the cool water on my toes, then my ankles, up to shins, up to knees, up to thighs, passing (aforementioned) genitalia, tickling my belly, wetting my sparse armpit hair, up to the neck, and then dive, dive, dive, into the froth, into the familiar cuddle of the water, sweet, sweet, deep water... Oh, how I adore the sea, like a passionate lover pursues his pursued, like a jealous and over-zealous Romeo, jumping on his Juliet. Oh, how I love the sea. And then some toss-pot lifeguard whistled and waved at me to come back in, oh well, a glimpse of glory, a brief blast of beauty. And perhaps a taster of things to come...

But before that, before then, today to tell you about. Two meagre hours of work, talking slowly to shy Saudi teenagers, to vaguely (but only vaguely) amused Vietnamese, and a pleasant young fellow named Y__ Y_____, you remember him, don't you? Breakfasting with Oma and Ma, then a bit of boxing (watching, not participating). Then, by car, to a lake. I stripped off, unequipped with towel or trunks, but what's a little nudity between Bavarian neighbours? Same trusty trunks on, and then a brisk jog to the water, making a brave face of it (I had to, people were looking), and then splash, breast-stroking for all I was worth. The small amusement and novelty of watching or seeing their husband/son-in-law/Dadda flop into the lake over, you three went for a more sensible walk *around* the lake. Leaving me, but leaving me with the best view of the panoramic mountains, and the green pastures on and beyond them. A view of heaven, from a cold lake. Not quite the salty sea of Rome's Mediterranean, but nevertheless, wonderful. And if I sound or seem to you like a fool for almost frothing at the mouth about a mere dip in the sea or a lake, then I do not apologize, for this is the lesson, daughter: Find your joys, and savour them when you discover them. Or go look for them if they are not appearing. For life is short, and smiles don't come with guaranteed returns. And hey, swimming is good for you, too.

As is reading. Whether this shambling and nonsensical 'book', or anything that might take your fancy. Please do, please try. I hope that one day, you won't bend book covers, as you do now, or chew on the pages instead of reading them. If you do this still in adulthood, I should warn you, it may be perceived as a little 'eccentric'.

Briefly, I promise, briefly... After a lovely spate recently of devouring classic novels, I'm currently abstaining by instead reading a non-fiction classic, 'In Cold Blood'. It's about a murder of a family. Jolly, yes. The writer talked to the parents of the murderers, and it occurred to me that I could as easily be the parent of a victim, as of a perpetrator. Obviously, I do hope to be neither. However, the interviews do show that a parent's influence does have its limits. Or so it seems to me. We can try to keep our kids' dainty little fingers from being shut in doors, we can take away the things from them that they shouldn't have, we can even resemble the sainted examples we have known in the past, and produce kind, polite, super-duper-trooper bambinos... But if? But what if? Some cheesy bugger once told me that 'if' is the central part of 'life'. How great, but how daunting it is, then, that the cheesy bugger had it all completely and utterly spot-on.

But relentlessly, we shall continue, brave and unbound, and the sun will glimmer off the water on our backs.
To which, the matter before us... One big 'if' has finally been marvellously answered. I refer to the lovely fact that in between ten and twenty days, we, my dear, shall be hot-footing it off to Tunis, Tunisia. Yes, it has finally been confirmed. And it is my cheerful duty to report this to you, dear daughter of mine. For nine or ten (or more) months, we will be living in the land of Hannibal, quite literally in Carthage (or a town with the same name as the ancient empire). We'll even have our own swimming pool

to splash and frolic in. It shall be most good, little one, I imagine. I hope.

Finally, the sun, the yoke, has gone down, its work for the day done. It gently flopped down onto the land, leaving a slight sunset as its humble farewell. The dark and graceful trees were not alone for too long though, as their good friend, the moon, came out to greet them cordially. Its universal language appreciated by all and sundry surrounding them. With the sight of their chum, the sun, gone, the strong trees said goodbye to the day, and hello to the night's messenger. That kind moon, up there, hanging in the heavens, it lights the way for weary travellers, who move in the darkness.

But we shall travel no more tonight, little one. Our recent past, like the sun, shines bright, and it has left quite a nice subtle sunset, as I have tried my best to describe to you, in these pages. But now the time has come for the moon, and the little girl who carries its light so gracefully must prepare to see her dreams. It's late, you should get your rest. And so should all of the Daddies, especially those who have earnt it. Good night, little one. Little one, you.

Nineteen

The Little Mouse

Finally, finally here. In this big room. Sweating and sweaty, on my own again, no noise but the whirring of the hard-working fan, chugging, working overtime. Five big wind chimes are opposite me, I half expect them to start moving, and to start to make their peculiar clunky music. But there is no wind, no air. Also, a big mirror, I see a man in it with thin arms, long black hair, tired eyes, masks in front of him. I see a door with 'Amour' on it, and an old hanging of some sort. I see a face mask, still needed sometimes, hanging on the door. I see the suntan lotion bottle, that we use for you alone. In fact, just ten minutes ago, I was putting little splodges of it on my fingers, and then onto your face. Your expressions change while I carry out this daily procedure, at first unsure, then slightly put-out, or even annoyed, then starting to accept it, as if remembering that it's okay, it's not too bad, and then almost a flicker of enjoyment, as I move your small rubbery cheeks, dab more on your nose, wipe your forehead so that it's covered too, flup your bottom lip to finish, and then it's done. You give me a little crafty smile afterwards. Your smiles seem to have a wonderful amount of expressions and meanings. Your Ma came through the door to join us, hair still wet from the shower, white heels clicking, as they took you, to church, in the centre, via the train. In the heat. This heat is nothing to joke about, it feels oppressive this morning, hence the whirring, blowing, old hearing-aid coloured fan, up there, above 'Amour'.

Rewind. Nearly three weeks back. To another little mouse.
We finally got the go-ahead, the push out of the starting blocks that we had been waiting for. For months. They finally said 'You can come now'. So we went, or tried to. But first, another rental van, to move our things from Röthenbach to Oma's big loft. I think it was all going pretty okay. Until the washing machine. I'm still not completely sure how we got it out of the bathroom, through the door. Did we take something off? Or turn it around? Or upside down? Or…? We knew it was going to be heavy. I had seen two rather strange, atrociously smelling men from the electric company deliver it to us. I saw them struggle, but from a slight distance, such was their pong. They must have had a hard time. But your Ma and I are extreme optimists, occasionally. Brave as lions, blind as bats. But we did, we got it out, through the door, albeit with scratches to everything, including ourselves. It was on the edge of the stairs, then we lifted, still fairly polite to each other at this point in the day, polite, but both impatient, wanting so much for things to go well, so much so that I just knew that the rising emotions and tempers wouldn't always go unchecked, blustering around us. But, it was up, and I had it, and your Ma had it, and we were 'slowly, slowly…' taking it down the stairs. Until your Ma said stop. And so, we stopped. We put it down, carefully. And I took the weight. Your Ma shouted first.
"A mouse! A mouse!".
She wailed, she screeched. Maybe I turned just half an inch, maybe I didn't, but I did see a small dark pile next to us. The washing machine slid, or moved slightly. Onto your Ma's foot.

"Aaargh!"
"Are you okay? Are you okay?"
"Why did you move? Why did you move?"
We seemed to be speaking in pairs of questions.
"Can you move it?" No reply. Maybe a wiggle of a little toe.
"Can you move it?".
She could, she did. Relief. And then back to the unusual issue of having a farm animal on our staircase. It was a mouse. How did it get there? No idea. The pipe of the washing machine was dripping water, the weight seemed to increase. We lifted again. Turned, pivoted, slowly, slowly, around the corner and down, down, down. A rest. Foot okay, but a mouse deceased. We still had to take it down more stairs, and then onto the van. That was how I hurt my arms, and gave myself enough damage to feel ill and tired for three or four days afterwards. That, plus walking up and down four flights of stairs with everything else that was in the van. The piano was easy compared to the sodding washing machine. But I survived. The mouse did not. That poor corpse, without a name, had squeaked its last squeak. And it met a sad watery toilet grave, at my callous aching hands.

The Unexpected Camels

Or were they dromedaries? Do I even know the difference? The next day while we still had the van, we were asked ('tasked' is a better word for it) by our neighbour/landlady to disperse of her old cupboard, and to pick up a new one. No problem, we said, unknowingly and naively, as it turned out. The night before, I was summoned, still weary from the washing machine-piano-mouse-boxes-lifting-thing, to help her with something. "Okay", I mumbled, and trudged down those damned steep metal steps. The task was to take apart a big bookcase, about thirty parts, up her basement stairs, and into the garden, ready for us to take the next day. Just what I needed. I must have slept very soundly that night.

The next day we took it to an odd pair of blokes, near to us. Or was it the same day? Maybe we... Yes, we did. We put it in the van. These events are extremely confused in my mind right now, as I sit at a table, three weeks later, on another continent. Did we do that the same day as the washing machine fiasco? Yes, I think we did.

The two strange men took the pieces of the mammoth book case. Then we took everything else to Oma's, to unload it there. Everything up to the loft, except for the piano and the infernal washing machine, which went in the basement. And then one more task, to pick up the replacement (plus taking the van back). In the meantime, flights were booked, the green light had been given. So that added yet another task, to get our remaining things and to leave the house. We drove in the empty van, drove some more, through winding Bavarian country roads, up and down hills, until eventually arriving at *the house*. A young friendly heavily bearded man came out. He said that we should follow him. Okay, we said, confused. He got on his little push-bike and rode on, to show us the way to 'the thing', 'the cupboard'. We followed him in this way for about five minutes. Us in the rental van, and him, steadily pedalling on his little bike. And what he led us to... Was a camel farm.

For a moment, I felt like I had slipped into a peculiar dream. You might expect horses, cows, or even sheep in an area like that. You might. But you wouldn't expect six camels (or dromedaries), with pretty eyelashes, looking at you, with an equal amount of common curiosity. I suppose they don't see many English-Persians, or little Roman babies either...

The 'thing', the 'cupboard' wasn't a cupboard at all, nor was it a bookshelf. It was, instead, thirty big heavy dark-blue pieces of something. The beardy on the bike bid us a hasty farewell, telling us that someone would come and help us. And so he did, a slightly annoyed farmer in a cowboy hat. Who seemed very particular about how each piece should be placed in *our* van. When we finally got it all back to the landlady, it wasn't at all what she wanted. I am still not entirely sure what that thing was. Suffice to say, and I think it was all the same day, it was all a gigantic and tiring waste of time. Apart from the camels. When you were sat on the farm floor, in your car seat, you peaked at them, with a somewhat detached interest. And maybe even a world-weary look in your eyes, which belied your years, which said "Yep. Okay. Camels. Right...".

The next day, we (definitely) went to the airport, with eight or nine pieces of luggage, on two trains, pushing you, in a car seat, on top of a pushchair, with one hand. Your Uncle met us there, he got drinks for us while we queued, it was short but extremely slow-moving, in a different place to where the information board told us it would be. It felt rushed, strange. Every single one of the people in front of us seemed to take an age. The young couple, the big American lady with a suitcase full of Haribos and Rittersports, which she had to completely repack. We waited...

We couldn't get on the flight. We hadn't taken corona tests. We remonstrated, oh, how we remonstrated. "But the German government says this... the Tunisian government says that... The U.N. says...". They didn't really care. They only said "Air France says...", and that was all that mattered. The supervisor came, and tried to call France. It was as good as calling Jupiter, with a Nokia 3210, with half a bar's battery left. Your Ma got upset, I got angry, your Uncle wondered why we weren't drinking the cappuccinos. A lot of talking, a lot of back and forth, but ultimately, all of it in vain. We took our ten tonnes of luggage (and you, a bemused baby) back to Röthenbach, in your Uncle's electric car. We stopped at his place on the way back. He went out for a haircut. And while we waited for him in his very non-child safe apartment, at that moment, I must have said 'No' to you, for everything. Wires and electrical things and cables and plants and food wrappers. No, no, no. Meanwhile, your poor Ma was trying to talk to someone with a modicum of decency from the travel agency. She must have spent about seven hours on hold... No, it most certainly was not a marvellous couple of days...

The Fast Turtle

We finally flew, I think, four or five days later. Nuremburg to Paris to Tunis. Not before proving that we didn't all have the coronavirus, by letting two nurses in a carpark put something up our noses, and then in the backs of our throats, and paying a small fortune for it.

After four hours at Charles De Gaulle airport, it was finally time to go. Thus beginning the start of your superstardom here. I do recall thinking that it was slightly unusual, when a pretty little Tunisian girl, sitting next to you on the second flight, was extremely patient with you tapping her, and staring at her for a few hours. Well, it turns out that white-blonde babies are, to many Tunisians, very interesting, very unusual, very wanted. People don't merely stare at you here, oh no. They touch you, they pick you up, they kiss you, they squeeze your cheeks, they blow you kisses. They even follow you. Even teenage boys, usually way too cool for school, go all gooey eyed at you. Old men too, pull every face they can muster to entertain you, to perhaps bring about a smile. From Princess Emily. My reactions range from pride, to annoyance, passing through the usual reaction, which is to smile back, and then hope that they go away after a bit. If Tunisian kids all had blonde hair and pale skin, would *they* all be so adored? Personally, I find the people here very attractive. The girls, the boys, the proud old men, the life and soul behind the eyes of their women. They seem to see only you though, and I must learn to live with it.

Your Ma has been working from home here. And the reason for this, again, is the coronavirus. They haven't let her go to the office yet, thus far, because she can't take another test to prove that she hasn't caught it since the last test. And if that doesn't make much sense to you, then trust me, it makes even less to me. So we have lunch together, at this new home, sometimes followed by a swim. I swear your Ma must have the eyes of a particularly attentive eagle sometimes. While we were flopping around in the swimming pool, she spotted a tiny, tiny turtle, one afternoon last week. It was roughly the size of a large dog turd, approximately. Still, she saw it, in our big lovely garden. Straightaway, she ran in to get her camera, and you were shown him (we think that it's a he). We named him after a friend of ours who once said that you have a face like a turtle (he said it's okay because he himself has a 'sack-face'…). The excitement passed, and as we said our Au-revoirs, we felt sure, completely sure, that we would see him again. Alas, we have not. As this intrepid exploring turtle seems to be significantly swifter than the average turtle. He's gone, gallivanting somewhere, god bless him.

The Kittens

So your Ma is at home from Monday to Friday, either in the bedroom or in the kitchen, beavering away on her laptop, working on various projects to eventually, hopefully, help people here, or in this region. As seems par for the course with her current employers, her team seems to be an interesting bag of characters, with strange names and stranger habits. I leave her to it, to negotiate this phase, on her own. I understand little of it, and can assist her, only with the occasional bit of English language advice. Everything else, she does alone, and her team of slightly unhelpful miscreants seem more intent on putting up new barriers, than on pushing her over the ones already there. Or so it seems to me...

All of which leaves me with you, or you with me. This is what we do. We have breakfast with your Ma, after you wake at seven or eight. I will myself out of bed, and prepare something, like banana or apple with porridge or millet. We eat with your Ma, or rather, your Ma and I eat, and sip our coffees, in-between trying to feed you. You don't like the high-chair much. At around nine, your Ma hides herself away and starts her graft. Maybe a nappy change, a drop or two of water, a bit more food, plus the aforementioned ritual of the suntan lotion, a dress, socks to keep your feet covered (your legs have a slight tan already), and all topped off with the hair-tie. I could write a novel (comparable in length to 'A' la recherche du temps perdu') just about your hair-ties, and how putting them on gives me such immense satisfaction, or torture (and you too, squirming and completely un-cooperative, or placid and delightful). Then out we go, into the big wide world. Hot, dusty, litter-covered streets surround us. The pot-holes and various discrepancies in the road can only remind us of Rome. To the train station we go, not 'our' station, that one's closed, but to the next one, Carthage Dermech, up the hill, around the corner, the one on the right. Purchase a very cheap ticket (roughly fifteen pence), and away we go, passing your adoring public, left, right, and centre. As we wait for the train, I try to put in your mouth as much of the remaining breakfast as I can. Which so far has taken us to the sea, many mosques, many cafés, many sights worth seeing. Bookshops for me to peruse, and people for you to be admired by. The sights in this town alone, Carthage, have filled the pages of countless history books, as this is the home, the fort, of Hannibal. He of the elephants, he of the Punic wars, fought against your fellow Romans.

How lucky we are to be slap-bang in the middle of the train route, which takes us one way, to the beach town of La Marsa, and to the other, which is Tunis centre. Through the blue and white calm of Sidi Bou Said, through the hectic streets of La Goulette, past the airport, to destinations as yet unknown. It's a hell of a place, and about the same temperature too.

We only stay out for three or four hours, getting off the train, by the supermarket, so the checkout ladies can adore you some more, and I can buy pop, biscuits, and various other melting things. Then slowly stumble home, sweat pouring. You stop and wave at all of the kittens, and there are many. Alive, they seem skinny, malnourished, not too wary, interested in us, like their human counterparts. Tunis' humans and cats adore you. One or two dead poor little moggies, though, eyes bulging, and faeces still being extracted, unbelievably sad and forlorn. Why did no one help them? The sheer number of tiny felines means, I suppose, the occasional deceased one. Slain by the heat or a lack of food, I don't know. Poor creatures.

Of which troubling thoughts seem very far away, when I dip into the pool. Our pool, the pool we splish in, we splash in. Did I mention that we have our own swimming pool? Surely a working class Northern European's dream is to have his or her own swimming pool, in a warmer climate. Sometimes I go in alone, to cool down, and sometimes (I'm sorry to report, but I've only done it once or twice or thrice...) in 'the state of nature', nude as the day *I* was born. You don't care. You watch me frolic, I pretend to be a shark, or I make dolphin noises. Acting the fool for your enjoyment, being paid in giggles and chuckles, a most fortunate payment indeed. Sometimes, you come in with me, and your Ma, in your 'swim nappy', worn under your turquoise and pink swimming costume. You eye the aqua with your inquisitive eyes, holding onto us, unsure until we fool around and make you feel secure again. A smile to begin with, and then on the road to safety and security. You seem to hold it against the pool water, when you thump it, and it has the audacity to foist water upon your face, most unpleasantly. You haven't quite figured that one out yet. Your unknowingness, and lack of comprehension, sometimes, is wonderful.

Lunch for us means waiting for lunch for you, which then means a need for patience on our part, spoon by spoon you get to the bottom of the jar or the dish, gollop by gollop it goes down. When it's not going in your hair, or elsewhere, as is often the case.

Then we play outside, or inside, with something. Lately, with building blocks which would be better described as destruction blocks, as you seem to take way more pleasure in knocking them down than in building anything. Books you glance at, or try to mangle. The four-coloured rings you still love, a yellow wooden car, which I think I might like more than you do. All of these things, and more, pass the time until your Ma is back from the bedroom. Your dear sweet Mama, who has milk **in** her, and who can console you like I cannot. We tell ourselves that we are a team. I suppose we are.

The Fish and The Gecko

Yesterday, or two days ago, she told me that she hadn't yet got an idea of the culture here, or a solid impression of the people, or of how things really are. It is a shame really that we can go out every day, to explore, to discover, and she cannot, being as she is, tied to the work. The work that, let us not forget, is keeping us here, on this grand adventure. I told her that these are *my* impressions: the friendly people, the boiling afternoons, the cooler evenings, the spicy food, the mint tea, the calm drivers, the holes in the pavements, the dust, the dates, the desire of the people to take life as it comes, as it is, and not how they desire it to be, the cries of the minarets, blue and white buildings everywhere, Hannibal and history, couscous, cheap cabs, and kittens, the dead and the alive, the living and the dying...

Plenty of fish in the sea, but some with their bones in the streets, that we left for the cats' pleasure. The scales cut off, the head removed, the tail carved with care, off. Entrails, grey and bloody at the same time, all for the cats of Carthage Byrsa. All except what we had on our forks.

The gecko was by the pool, smiling and being admired, complete and almost alive one day. Dead, completely dead, and stripped by the ants the next. More bones. Fish bones, gecko bones, inside and outside our home. The kittens will be merely bones too, but then so shall we. It's not so bad. We are all creatures under the sun, and I am no better than a cat, or a fish, or a lizard, or even a hungry ant. If anything, us humans are the worst. If anything...

The Sparrow

'Spatz' as your Ma calls you. Her little sparrow. You're not the worst of anything. I told your Ma one day recently that I hope we are doing what is best for you, the right things for you, with you, by you. It's only because I care about you.

I am still at the table, looking at 'Amour', and me, the dark man in the mirror. You could be in a church, or in the middle of a soukh, I don't know. On the way home, to this, our new home. Either way, you are in Tunisia. And believe me, my little creature, it sure has been a long way getting here.

Twenty

<u>One today</u>

Home (1)

One today
And just ate two bites, did three steps, and said 'Dadda' four times
Played with a brush while I squashed a cockroach
Our hair the same length, yours golden-blonde-brown, mine black-brown-grey
We're at a table, your sleeping Ma
Bought you a sunflower and a rose
Yellow and white, like parakeets in Rome
The little Roman E.S.C. is one today
"One more bite, it's the last one, promise"
I lie to you on your birthday
You woke at six, kicked us five times
For our lies, impatience, harsh words, silly sometimes
The cake is down the road, probably
The DVDs will be taken out and scattered asunder from the shelf
The foot will be removed from the drum
Sleeping Mama will wake soon
Muddy coffee will need to be made
'Du Maus' gets a birthday song now
'Der Spatz' is getting a birthday poem now
'Du Dieb' is going to put her hand in a socket
Mama dreamt of cockroaches, she told me
You dream of marshmallows, I tell me

Pink shining clouds, which will have milk inside
Falling, slowly and steadily, for eternity
Into your mouth
Which has six teeth, five smiles, only two lips
But four DVDs are being pulled out again, pelted around
And the rings are being thrown around
Red, blue, green rings
Yellow hair on your head
DVDs opening, more and more than four
'Bang, bang' goes the drum, mischievous tinker
A rascally rabbit –
Is one today.

One today
The pink polo Turkish low-cost Lacoste rip-off
I wore this day, last year, when you...
(not 'arrived' because that sounds like a train or a plane...)
When you were born, birthed, burped, brought into this universe
World, earth, city of Caesar, that Rome home. Remember?
One year later, you are being dressed in new clothes, pretty, pretty
While I still kill cockroaches
While messages for you come in
From England and Germany
And now we're going out for breakfast, it's balmy, barmy really
But now we're not because breakfast hasn't been made for you
And I can't find the chopping board because someone has hidden it
And didn't cut the apple properly because I'm clumsy
And hands smell of apple and a hot morning and a hot sun

Is waiting, sneakily, out there, for us, the weasel
Waiting to pounce, like those suns before did
While the apple boils, while the town burns
While you are in another room
While the thought occurs, dripping into my mind
That one day soon, you will have cracked heels too
And a bad knee and lank hair, and scars
Pink, on your finger, on your chin, on your belly
If you are like me. If you are like me, I hope you'll
Have suns to warm you, and not complaints
While apples boil, while clothes are put on
I can hear you, you're getting closer
Like a shark with only six teeth
Sweating, shouting, gesticulating, in new clothes
You, who is one today
I can't believe it
Or anything
Except the cockroach blood I wipe up
And the hot apple sauce on my hands

Train Station (2)

You snooze while we wait for the dirty train
With six blonde hairs
Covering two blue eyes
Ten toes tap slightly, silently
Ten fingers twitch, occasionally
One dimple can't be seen, so
One brain dreams of past lives, or future lives
Of adulthood and angst and ears pierced and nails painted
And the moon bigger than all of us, still

We're going to La Marsa
With Tunisians, loud, loud, excitable teens
A boy bangs an empty bottle with a stick

He's sixteen, or seventeen, simple, simple
Silly boys
The girls are quiet, watching, wary, pensive
The Mother's head covered, the girl has a piercing
The boys just get stupider
The Fathers, I suppose, are working and/or worrying.

Not this one
Not this day
He's just watching ten things, or two things
A one-year-old Daddy too, today
Enough apple in belly, enough water slipped or slurped
Not enough sleep for me, or you, little one, but
A middle aged man in a pink shirt
And a sleeping, snoozing, slightly snoring
Otherwise silent, Salome'
Waiting, no worries.
One year old today.
And the train comes.

Park (3)

The sad-faced, massive-nosed man
On the train
He knows it
The baggy-eyed, fake Prada princess
With moles and big earrings (and dreams too)
She knows it
The robin that is my Granddad
In winter, when the trees sob
Where it's too cold (but it's hot here)
He knows it
The sailor with the tattoo
That is my other Granddad
Has been gone to sea, a long time now
And he knows it

Your namesake, who could black an eye with a hug
And my Ma's Ma, who was short and golden and now sleeps too
They know it
The Palestinian, and all of the parents of your parents' parents,
All of them
The Iranian, the English, the Germans
And the fly on my hand, and the bee in my bonnet
The lady with young eyes, and eighty years at least
Who cleans the streets with water and a smile
They all know it too
The birds in the palm trees can't deny it
The rats by the road rarely forget it
The cat said, even when dead
What the dog heard, happy and fed
The old and the young
The weak and the strong
They all know it.
That –
My daughter is one today
One year old
One year young.
With a candle and a cake
And a world and a whisper.

Fin.

Printed in Great Britain
by Amazon